Mike & Judy

MISSION MEMORIES

World War II

MISSION

MEMORIES

World War II

Theodore Homdrom

[signature: Teddy Homdrom]

12.12.02

Homdrom, Theodore
  Mission Memories: World War II / Theodore Homdrom
1.   History – World War II.

First Printing July 2002

Printed in the U.S.A.

To order copies, contact:
Theodore Homdrom
1544 Fulham Street
Saint Paul, MN 55108

CONTENTS

Introduction

I didn't ever foresee that I would write anything about my military experiences, but I've been urged to do so from several different sources. At the funeral of my cousin Harold Vollen in June 1998, my memory was jolted back to a family reunion a few years earlier when he specifically asked me: "Ted, you must write about your war experiences – at least for us family members." I felt badly that I had failed him, but I still felt that I didn't have time to tackle such a task.

Sometime in late 1997 I received a phone call from Jim Liddle, the pilot on the original Flying Fortress crew with which I went overseas. A friend of his had traced me on the Internet. What a surprise to hear from him after nearly 54 years! In November 1998 my wife, Betty, and I flew to Dallas for this much-anticipated reunion with him and his wife, Mary, and our ball turret gunner, Jack Burke. The reminiscing from each of us was really lively and quite emotional. Jim had several books and mementos while Jack sent me his photograph album and several books. I had brought along my old writing pad blotter on which I had listed the dates[1], target, name of pilot and memos of each of my 30 bombing missions. As Jim and Jack were eager to have such a record, each received a photocopy of it. They also urged us to come to Houston, Texas, for the 1999 Reunion of the 381st Bomb Group. It was a thrill to meet several others whom I hadn't seen for over 55 years. I found more material for my undertaking. It also brought back many memories.

When I had all this additional information and my volunteer work gave me a gap, I decided that I'd better make an effort to complete these Mission Memories.

After an Honorable Discharge from military service, I was very reluctant to talk about what I had gone through. Whenever I was somehow lured into conversation about a certain mission, I found that in the reliving of that experience, it became too emotional, making it difficult to fall asleep that night. Consequently, I felt it was wiser to concentrate on the present and the future.

Steve Hutchinson, Mercedes Alcala Galan, Betty Homdrom, Ev Hanson and Victor Hanson encouraged me enthusiastically and provided technical assistance and constructive criticism.

But how did I get involved in war in the first place? Having graduated with a BA from Concordia College in Moorhead, Minnesota, in May 1941, I obtained a position as a teacher and basketball coach in a small high school in Comertown, Montana. Little did I ever imagine that as I was teaching history that the Japanese would attack the United States at Pearl Harbor on December 7, that same fall. As happened to most men after the total mobilization, I, too, would receive a letter of "Greetings" from President Roosevelt!

In quick order I had to leave my teaching, head for home and, as ordered by the Draft Board, report by March 1942 for induction as a private in the US Army at Fort Snelling, Minnesota. During our induction, we began to become accustomed to crude or even shocking remarks by veteran non-commissioned officers. When we were issued dog-tags in duplicate on our string around our neck, some recruit asked, "Why two?" the veteran answered, "Well, when you're killed, they'll take one and leave the other one on your body." One World War I veteran urged us regarding the danger of venereal disease, which he referred to as "the clap". He related an incident in that war. A soldier having caught the clap was asked about the circumstances. He replied, "I caught it in the toilet." His medical officer curtly retorted, "That's a heck of a place to take a girl!" It didn't take us long to become accustomed to rough talk of all sorts.

Having scored quite high in the Mechanical Aptitude test at this induction center, I was assigned to the newly developing 5th Armored Division stationed at Camp Cooke, California. I was happy that at least I wasn't assigned to the infantry!

PHASES OF TRAINING

5th Armored Division

Basic Training

Although this strange period of my life could cover at least a chapter, I will confine it to the progress I made as a soldier leading up to how I ended up in the U.S. Army Air Corps.

After the long and interesting train ride, seeing for the first time such things as oil wells in Oklahoma, the Arizona desert, New Mexico cactus, pueblo villages, and the orange groves of California. I remember telling one of the fellows in my car, "I wish the train would stop so we can see whether or not those are Sunkist oranges!" Without a sense of humor, I don't think I could have survived as well as I did in the service. We arrived at last at Camp Cooke.

Having been assigned to Company D, I found the orientation had too much emphasis on unnecessary details such as how to shine one's shoes and how to prepare for Saturday inspections. After spending the first four Sundays on Sunday KP (kitchen police) for failing to pass the inspections, I finally decided to comply with these inessential regulations. My superiors were pleased when they noticed my improved demeanor.

In basic training I learned all about several types of guns and how to shoot them. Although I had never fired a 45-caliber pistol before, I absorbed all that the instructor told us, including the hold on the gun, breathing and how to bring it down to squeeze the trigger. When we got to the firing range, I received the highest score – 49 out of a possible 50. The company commander then called me in, asking if I would like to go to Officers' Training School. I declined, saying "I don't want to become a 90-day wonder", the description we had for some of our officers.

After receiving my license for the jeep, I became the driver for the company commander. As I had been issued a pistol with ammunition, he told me on payday to "shoot anyone who monkeys with us". I also passed the driver's test for 6X6 trucks, half-tracks and light and medium tanks. Having become competent at double clutching hauling grain through the Badlands of Western North Dakota the previous summers, I really enjoyed driving all the army vehicles. One of my buddies called me "Old Smoothie".

When I was nearly through basic training, I had a 24-hour pass and went to Santa Barbara. After attending church services and walking downtown on my own for dinner, I was picked up by a family who had seen me in church.

It turned out that I had dinner with this Johnson family and continued being with them the rest of the day and evening. Their daughter Jeanette took me sightseeing as well as swimming in the Pacific. I left them with a standing invitation to return whenever I could. It certainly had become a wonderful break to be with a family again and, of course, their lovely daughter!

That interlude happened while I was becoming a bit wary of the correspondence with a former girlfriend from college. Estelle was urging me to go to officers' training so that she, I felt, hopefully would not just be married to an ordinary soldier. I wrote telling her that I believed we ought to lay off writing a while to see how much we would miss each other. I certainly didn't feel this was the time to plan for marriage.

Back at camp I merely kept doing the best that I was able to do. Our softball team, of which I was the pitcher, only lost in the regional championship game. Although I really enjoyed driving the tank, I felt honored that I was chosen to be a tank commander. On July 1st, my birthday, I was promoted, with a few others in my company, to the rank of PFC. The training my crew and I received was geared more to resemble combat conditions. For this training, the ideal location to simulate northern Africa would be the California desert.

Light tank crew: Tank Commander Homdrom, Johnson, Hagman, Dreibelbeis

A few of us from each company were chosen to establish the camp in an area that was very wild with only sand and scrub brush somewhere near the Colorado River. Because of the extremely primitive conditions, we were informed about possible dangers, including the presence of rattlesnakes, which might be attracted by our warm bodies as we lay with our blankets and shelter half on the sand. Before I went to sleep, I attempted to form a mental image as to what I would do if this were to happen to me. At the same time, with only the stars above, I felt when I prayed that God was very near.

Just before dawn on the following morning, after rolling over on my side hoping to get a little more sleep, I felt something trying to pull out from under my arm. Immediately I knew what it was and realized I'd have to "beat him to the draw". Following my mental "programming" of the previous evening, I lay without moving a few moments and then all of a sudden sprang up before it could coil and strike. Lest the rattler were to get to the men lying all around on the ground, I rushed 20 feet away, grabbing the axe which we had used the evening before and which lay on top of our tank. Rushing back to where I had been sleeping, I bashed the snake right on my blanket. I then cut off the rattles, which I still have, as a souvenir.

The following evening everyone was reluctant to lie down. A few even chose to sleep in or on top of their tank. Because I was quite confident as to what to do if such an incident were to happen to me again, I was the first one to again stretch out on the sand. It's strange how I was remembered by that incident even two years later when I visited my old outfit after they arrived in England. What a wonderful reunion it was as I chatted with my old buddies in their barracks. Now being an officer, I couldn't eat with them. I had to eat with the officers. My old company commander, then Capt. Anderson but now a Lt. Col., also remembered the incident and introduced me as "the man who had slept with a rattle snake" to his fellow officers!

While on maneuvers, we had many experiences. In August I was promoted to corporal and the following month to sergeant. One Sunday, while a buddy of mine and I walked by our regimental headquarters, I saw a poster urging all who had good eyesight and at least two years of college to apply for the Air Corps. As I had seen the Air Corps A-20s flying so low over us, I thought that at least they were out of all of this dust. Consequently I obtained a form and applied.

In early November 1942, I had orders for an interview at March Field, California, which included both a physical and a mental examination for the Air Corps. I had a high score on the mental test and then continued with the physical in the afternoon. Due to my body having become accustomed to desert conditions, I was required to stay over until the next day for a recheck on my slightly high temperature and blood pressure. Fortunately those were normal the following day. I then hitchhiked back to the desert for continued maneuvers.

While waiting for any kind of reaction to my application, I continued on overnight problems and finally a 3-day problem resembling combat conditions as closely as possible. From these exercises – sometimes dashing on without supplies keeping up with us – I became accustomed to being hungry and thirsty. When I hear others even now saying that they are hungry or thirsty, I myself hardly discern any such craving.

I shall never forget the final night on the desert. Our tanks and all of our equipment had been sent on ahead on flat cars. Told that we should make the best of it, we were only left with our two blankets and a shelter half. When the sun sets, it's cold enough on the sand in late November, but on this night there was a cold northwest wind and constantly blowing sand. A buddy and I put our shelter halves together as a pup tent and lying together with our clothes on with our blankets below and on top of us we were bitterly cold. We were happy the next day to be returning to our comfortable barracks near the Pacific Ocean.

After a few days back at Camp Cooke, I was given a 2-day pass to go again to March Field, California, for a personal interview. The first evening in Hollywood gave me a chance to visit with Cousin Goodie Landsverk. After securing a hotel room, I visited the Hollywood canteen, which entertained military personnel royally. At the counter we were given sandwiches, cake, coffee, milk, cigarettes (for those who smoked) and even souvenirs.

At March Field the next day the Aviation Cadet Board asked me about my education, background, and even whether I had dates very often! I replied, "yes, sir, anytime I can get a pass." Smiling their approval, they asked me to wait in the next room until all of us who had been interviewed were called in. Only one failed to pass the Board's scrutiny.

On my return to camp, I went via Santa Barbara to see Jeanette; obviously I was living up to what I had told the Board about dates! I had also been advised by the Board to take a leave home, if possible, but all I could obtain was a 3-day pass. Again I had a nice visit with cousin Goodie in Hollywood. My brother Clarence also obtained a pass so we could stay together. Johnsons also came. Among other things we did was to bowl at the 52-Lane Bowling Alley, take rides at the carnival and attend church.

Returning to camp on December 2, I was told that the Adjutant had been looking for me. At Regimental Headquarters, he told me to get all of my affairs with the company straightened out and leave that night.

It was very difficult for me to make such a sudden break with my buddies with whom I had trained for combat the past nine months. Firm friendships had been established; we had gone through many experiences, some dangerous, together. To mention one: one of the five on my medium tank crew, John Krull, had drowned while attempting to drive our tank on a pontoon bridge across the raging Colorado River. Not knowing whether we would ever see one another again, we all wished each other well in our own respective areas of service through the war.

Army Air Corps

Nashville, Tennessee

The trip by Southern Pacific went as close to Mexico as half a mile at El Paso, Texas. Not being able to get a berth, I had to sit up, but I wrote home that I lived very well – being allowed $1 per meal!

When the train stopped a day at New Orleans, I visited the places of historical interest, thinking this might help me if I ever went back to teaching history. I found it to be a fascinating place in so many ways.

Again, after a sleepless but enjoyable night playing games with newfound friends on the train, we arrived at Nashville, Tennessee. I found the place very gloomy. The ground was slushy and muddy, the sky was cloudy, and the old shacks for barracks left much to be desired. We were also under a 6-week quarantine.

After about a week of mostly lying around at the Aviation Cadet Classification Center in Nashville, reading or playing cards, we were finally told that we would be processed. Whatever GI Insurance we had would automatically change to a $10,000 policy without charge. After changing some clothes for new ones, we had a long walk, with all of our luggage, to a new and better area of the camp.

Those of us who had been non-commissioned officers from previous outfits and experiences were placed in charge of seeing to it that there was some order, such as doing some of the marching, some guard duty, and reporting to our commissioned officer each morning.

Before we began the various physical, psychological and mental tests, we had the chance of indicating whether we'd like to be pilots, navigators, bombardiers or meteorological officers. Being a history major with a considerable number of math courses, I thought navigation would be interesting and indicated that as my first choice. The tests showed that I was able to be a pilot and was classified as such. Consequently I was looking forward to being one. However, when an order arrived for 60 cadets to go to Monroe Navigation School, it could not be filled, because not many had been classified in that category. When I was called in and asked if I would still like to be a navigator, I said it would be OK, feeling that maybe it was meant to be that way – a choice I never regretted.

The train journey to Monroe by way of Kentucky and Arkansas was very dirty and tiresome. However, when we arrived at the Army Air Force Navigation School at Selman Field in Monroe, we were completely overwhelmed by the congeniality of all the officers and upperclassmen. Tours or hazing had been abolished at this base. The Commanding Officer considered us as men and wanted us to get the most out of the course. Actually, Selman Field was the only complete navigation training station, both pre-flight and advanced, in the entire country. Here a cadet could wind up with an officer's commission and navigation wings without transferring to another school.[2]

The living accommodations made us feel more like we were in college, with six cadets in a suite of rooms. Because I was a tall person yet able to take shorter (30-inch) steps when we marched, I was chosen as the guide sergeant of the first platoon when we marched. Occasionally I was asked to lead them in morning exercises. When the class before us graduated, I was the honor guard holding the American flag at the parade rest stance on the right side of the stage. Another cadet held the pre-flight school flag on the other side with an armed guard by each of us. Naturally we felt pretty cramped after standing in that one position without moving for the hour-long program.

The pre-flight course had such subjects as meteorology, the movement of heavenly bodies and basic calculations for the various types of navigation.

We learned how to calculate our position from practice with the sextant, the calculator and other navigational tools. Later in the course we had a session in the pressure chamber in order for the instructors to determine whether or not we were suitable for high-altitude flying. There was a special diet for that day. We had to avoid gas-producing foods. As the pressure in the tank decreased, the gases within the body expanded and one had to swallow occasionally in order to equalize the pressure in the ears. Having stayed at the 38,000 feet level for three hours, similar to flying in an unpressurized bomber, I was qualified to fly at any altitude.

I still remember one of the first statements an instructor made, "Gentlemen, remember that there is no such thing as an air pocket. It's simply convection currents." The study of the factors affecting the weather was very interesting. The fact that only two of the six of us in our suite were allowed to go on to the advanced navigation course showed how careful the Air Force was to have the most qualified personnel in each position on the aircraft.

It's very difficult for anyone now to believe that my first flight in an airplane was when I, with two other cadets, an instructor and pilot flew an actual navigation exercise! What we had learned about pilotage – matching what we saw on the ground, such as roads and cities with our maps – we now put into practice. We learned valuable tricks of how to calculate the wind force, such as observing the waves on the water. We couldn't be accurate without knowing the strength and direction of the wind. Later we had flights using radio beams, dead reckoning (setting the compass headings and estimated time of arrival from the predicted winds) and celestial or a combination of whatever was possible.

I think we all found that celestial navigation was the most frustrating. While we were shooting and recording the altitude of three stars, looking these up in our books and making 3-star fixes on our map, we were aware that the plane had moved a considerable distance. Because that complete exercise of shooting and calculating took about ten minutes, we then had to project our track from the last known position through our fix, thus establishing our speed, wind and heading and consequently make the necessary changes in our course to reach our destination. How I wished I had had this knowledge of the heavenly bodies and their constant movement while I had been on desert maneuvers. One can't help but realize how great God's creation is.

The final days before completing the advanced navigation course were quite exciting. We had to be measured and fitted for the various types of clothing worn by officers. After the hard work I was looking forward to a furlough at home, which I had left when drafted a year and a half earlier. Then also I wondered where I would be sent. Having heard so much about the Flying Fortress, I was pleased to receive orders to take a 15-day delay-en-route to meet my B-17 crew at Moses Lake, Washington. Finally on graduation day, August 14, 1943, the Commanding Officer issued me, and the other graduates, silver navigational wings and

2nd Lt. Bars declaring each of us "an officer and a gentleman"!

This new life as an officer was initially quite different. Whereas previously as enlisted men we were required to salute any officer, now we had to wait for the enlisted person to salute us before we saluted in return. Of course, if we approached an officer of higher rank, we had to salute him first. However, as the Air Corps personnel were more casual, we new officers became accustomed to the new status rather quickly.

Training for Bombing Missions

Although it was wonderful after nearly 18 months to be home in Minnesota again, I could sense some mixed emotions with my mother. She was indeed happy to have me home, but with all three of her sons and a son-in-law in the service, she also worried about our safety. Many servicemen were already being killed in Africa, Italy, over Europe and in the Pacific. Yet because it was a popular war against the Axis powers, she was, I believe, a bit proud that we were willing to serve our country. Several of the relatives who were unable to serve indicated then or later that they hoped that I would drop eggs on Hitler - or the "Jerries"!

Once again I was off on the train – to meet the crew with which I was to go overseas. The members were from all over the US, including a Hopi Indian from Arizona, who was the tail gunner. The only other Minnesotan was the bombardier, Patrick O'Phelan, a graduate of St. Thomas College in St. Paul.

Although Jim Liddle from Oklahoma was considerably younger, he had had some training as a pilot in single engine fighters such as the P-47. However, he had a wish to fly the twin engine fighter, the Lightning (P-38) and applied for further training in a multi-engine school. Because of the accelerated program for training bombing crews, he was placed instead in the 4-engine bracket. He intensely disliked these birds that he said flew like a truck, but he still believed he could make the B-17 do anything a fighter could! After a brief flight – my first in a Flying Fortress – we as a 10-member crew were sent by train to Kearney Air Force Base in Nebraska. Here we were to have a variety of training flights before being sent overseas for combat. Lt. Baker was the co-pilot. Other crew members were S/Sgt. Clinton Ward, radio operator; S/Sgt. Jack Burke, ball turret gunner; S/Sgt. Schmitt and S/Sgt. Matchem, waist gunners; and T/Sgt. T. Vanderzee, engineer.

One such training mission was very memorable for the crew. The pilot still needed a high-altitude formation flight; I needed a 1,000-mile celestial mission. The plane was to fly with at least one other Fortress at 20,000 ft. on a 3-legged flight to the Twin Cities, Peoria (Illinois) and back to Kearney. As our pilot couldn't locate the other B-17, he asked me if it would be OK if we flew at a more comfortable 10,000 ft. altitude. I replied that I was being tested also – even if I recorded air speed, it would be too low. "Well," he said, "then I'll increase the indicated speed from 155 to 175 miles per hour." Despite this alteration in the flight plan, my celestial work was perfect, hitting the Twin Cities at exactly my ETA (estimated time of arrival). I then gave him the heading for Peoria, but when Patrick mentioned that his girlfriend lived just below us near St. Thomas College in St. Paul, Jim said that we'd just go down to buzz her. Over Minneapolis I was looking up at the tallest building, the Foshay Tower! After buzzing her home, he again reached the 10,000-ft. altitude and took my heading to Peoria.

Shortly thereafter he turned over the flying to co-pilot Baker and went back to the radio room for a nap. After our engineer, T/Sgt. T. Vanderzee, took the pilot's seat, Baker also got sleepy and told him to fly the heading. Unfortunately, with his jerky handling of the plane, I found it impossible to get 3-star fixes, so I did a bit of alternate celestial navigation. Just shooting the North Star, I purposely gave a heading to the right of Peoria. Then when we reached the latitude of Peoria (and Polaris), we merely turned straight east to our destination. (A landfall like that is comparable to a pilot who sees the ground, purposely flying to one side of a city or airport and then turning in on the road, river, or railway track that leads into that place.) Our course had attempted to teach us to adapt when conditions were abnormal.

When Jim took over again on the new heading for the final leg of our 1,000-mile practice mission back to Kearney, he called me saying that it looked like the fuel was too low to make it back. Considering the extra fuel consumed by the increased speed and buzz job over St. Paul, it seemed very possible. He began the alternative heading that I then gave him for Des Moines, Iowa, and reported to the tower personnel there that the low fuel light was already blinking. He then told us that they, in turn, ordered him to take a heading to the airport at St. Joseph, Missouri.

Then began frantic activity after Jim ordered us to throw out the heavy practice bombs (I still wonder where they hit) and go to the radio room for a possible crash-landing. It seemed like an awfully long time we tensely waited. When he saw the airfield light ahead, he went right on in over the trees, applied maximum brake pressure and stopped just short of the fence! Little did we realize that it was only a Piper Cub field, which did not have the 100-octane fuel required by B-17 engines.

When the operations officer at Kearney answered our pilot's phone call, he must have wondered what this young talented pilot would do next. Only shortly before he had not fulfilled according to specifications a required over-water test on the Gulf of Mexico. He and the Commanding Officer arrived later that forenoon in a Fortress with a barrel of 100-octane gasoline, but they were determined to investigate the incident thoroughly. What did they find but that our plane had over 1,000 gallons in the wing-tip tanks! Of course, it was the ground crew, the flight engineer and the pilot's responsibility to go over the pre-flight checklist. Jim insisted that he had not been informed about the installation of these wing tip tanks. The question was what charge would be made against him. I believe it was the CO who felt he should be court-marshaled. However, after their own experience in landing at this small field, the other pleaded that the pilot had done such an amazing job in the night landing. Consequently, they arrived at a compromise: "Let's send them overseas!" That incident ended our stateside training with not the best recommendations. The question was: how would we fare in combat over Germany? At least we perhaps had had more varied experiences than most other crews.

Homdrom's original crew in combat overseas
US Air Force photo, reprinted with permission

On to the European Theatre of Operations

Not many days later we were off on the train to a staging camp near New York City. Although passes to the city were limited, we took chances on getting through the fence. The "Big Apple" was so alive compared to our stay at Kearney. Many of us also wondered if we would ever get back to America alive and so we risked getting caught without a pass. After all, the punishment could be that they would only be too happy to wash their hands of us and send us quickly on overseas – just as they had done at Kearney!

Not many days later, 90 crews were a small part of the horde of 20,000 passengers that embarked on the Queen Mary. In peacetime the limit had perhaps been 2,000. Being an officer, I shared an upper stateroom with 17 other officers on hammocks three deep in a room where previously only a couple or small family stayed. Besides that, because the air far below was so foul, four enlisted men would come up every night and sleep on the floor between us. During the war the German submarines sank hundreds of various kinds of boats with escort protection, but because of a possible speed of 40 knots, the Queen Mary went unescorted. What a prize it would have been! Our ocean liner zigzagged nearly every 10 minutes. Besides that, she sailed on a huge zigzag nearly down to the warm Azores and then nearly up to cold Iceland and still made a war-time record crossing to our deportation port in Great Britain in four days and 16 hours. Except for an air raid and quite a rough sea, which made many seasick, there had been no loss of life - unlike what could have been the case if the 90 relatively inexperienced crews had attempted to fly over in 90 separate Flying Fortresses. Trained skeleton crews of five men did this job of ferrying each new bomber across the Atlantic. Returning to the U.S. by ship or plane, they repeated the task again and again.

Shortly after disembarking at Liverpool, England, we had our Thanksgiving dinner out of the mess kits that we carried. I don't think the one dishing up the potatoes caught it when I asked him if these were Irish cobblers! This was one of the three kinds I knew from younger days when cutting seed potatoes on my uncle's farm.

A trip across England by train took us and several other crews to the Ridgewell 8th Air Force Base. After the many combat losses, this 381st Bomb Group was very happy to welcome us who had been assigned there as replacement crews.

Our orientation during the next few weeks included lectures on relevant subjects pertaining to living and flying conditions and on navigational aids such as the GEE-box. The GEE (Ground Electronic Equipment) Box is a marvelous navigational system because it is fast, accurate and easy to use. GEE charts are issued upon two or three sets of hyperbolic curves that are superimposed in separate colors. These curves show the difference in the arrival time of radio signals transmitted by a Master Station and then re-transmitted by a Slave Station. The GEE Box in the plane is itself a cathode ray tube which is used to measure the difference in the arrival time of these two signals. A sharp navigator is able in about half a minute to obtain a fix that is accurate to within 30 feet.

We were then sent to the Quartermaster Sergeant to draw equipment. What a pleasant surprise to find that he was Kristen Lebakken, from my home town. His mother was a good friend of my mother. Kristen issued us necessary items such as electrically heated flying suits and flying boots for the extremely cold unheated and unpressurized bombers at high altitude. He also found a leather jacket with a fur collar for me. It was very cold in our barracks. On one of our first nights I recall that we had no fuel for the pot bellied stove, so a couple of the fellows broke up a shelf on the wall for firewood! After that someone always seemed to scrounge up some wood or coal for each evening.

COMBAT MISSIONS

1st Mission – Calais, France: December 24, 1943

When our operations officer came to my bunk at 6:30 am on Christmas Eve and told me I was to fly with Lt. Emil Urban in Ship Number 067, I was both surprised and pleased. Surprised that I was not flying with the crew I came over with and yet pleased that I could get my first taste of combat with an experienced crew. There was also a shortage of navigators due to injuries, illness and death.

The traditional "two eggs on my plate" for those facing danger was welcome after the usual powdered egg fare. From breakfast we went to another building for our briefing. When we saw the Intelligence officer lifting the curtain for a mission merely across the English Channel to Calais, we breathed a sigh of relief. We were to go over in small nine-plane formations to try to destroy installations believed to be for initially launching V-1 bombs, Hitler's secret weapon, over England.

After the briefing and preparation of our navigation flight plan, we had to get into our electrically heated flying suits. Though we were not to fly too high for this mission, we could expect temperatures of over 40 degrees below (Fahrenheit and Centigrade are the same there).

While going out to the Fortress, I couldn't help but wonder what a mission over enemy territory would be like. After all, it could happen that we wouldn't return that day. As we accelerated down the runway with our bomb load I breathed, "Lord, I am in your hands", a prayer which ever after I prayed when taking off. I also had my New Testament in my shirt pocket.

As we reached about 12,000 ft., we had to put on our oxygen masks; our planes were neither heated nor pressurized like commercial aircraft. As the outside temperature was approximately 40 degrees below zero, it was good to feel the warmth of our heated suits. Following the advice in orientation, I was pleased that my hands remained warm enough with thin silk gloves, rather than heavy clumsy ones. Naturally I had to constantly manipulate my instruments and record flight details and all crew observations in my log as well as being ready at any time to fire my 50-caliber machine gun.

Entering the air space over Europe for the first time, I had feelings of wonder and awe. This was under the control of the German Reich. Would my participation in the war make any difference? Yes, I believed it would and I would do my part to the best of my ability. With such thoughts I recorded the time, place and altitude of entering this German-held territory on my navigator's log.

Because we had British Spitfire and US Thunderbolt escort for this short mission, we didn't observe any German fighters. However, the barrage of flak was very accurate. One of our planes had 200 holes. As the targets were camouflaged it was difficult to identify the installations. Finally on the third pass we were able to release our bombs and head back to our base.

From a book by Cliff T. Bishop, I learned that our 1st Division had dispatched 277 bombers for the eight construction sites that day.[3] As Intelligence had information that Germany was preparing some sites for a much more deadly weapon called the V-2 bomb, it was important to delay and possibly eliminate that threat. As rumors spread about this secret weapon, the crews began calling Pas de Calais the "rocket coast".[4]

One could wonder about what a person in the service would be thinking in such a strange situation. It's true that I had no family there – not even a card or gift that Christmas. I knew each future mission could mean injury or even death. And yet we also knew we had to defend our liberty against such tyranny. As I reflected that evening on my first mission, I felt thankful that I could be involved with so many others who were risking their lives. Also, having told the Lord as we took off that I was in his hands, I then, and as always after each mission, thanked him for seeing me through "this one". As I read the Christmas story in my Bible, I realized that I had all that I needed there for a true celebration of the season. It was a joy to read how the heavenly host announced this baby's arrival: "Glory to God in the highest, and on earth peace, good will toward men". We were there to help bring that to pass.

Fortunately the Air Force realized that we had to have some time off to ease the tension while on combat duty. I wrote home on January 6, 1944, that my bombardier, Patrick O'Phelan, and I obtained a pass and went to London. I wrote: "We saw the Tower of London, Number 10 Downing Street and the most beautiful of all, Westminster Abbey, which is over 800 years old and has all those important people buried there".

When we left our hotel for an evening movie, we had to watch carefully which way we went in order to retrace our steps later. Not only the enforced blackout but also the heavy fog limited our vision. In any case it was good to get out of the very cool hotel room. One certainly was made aware of the strict security procedures and rationing. Air raids were frequent; however, we flying personnel usually ignored them, especially after warming up our beds.

Though I had made a start with only one mission in 1943, I was made aware of a change of leadership at year's end for the 381st Bomb Group. Col. Joseph Nazarro had been the leader of the organization from its beginning in the States. He left for a higher command and was promoted to General. Our new Group CO was Col. Harry Leber, Jr. from the beginning of 1944.[5] Col. Nazarro had made the outfit into an efficient bombing force with a record as one of the top groups in the 8th Air Force.

One standing rule that he made for our 381st Bomb Group was that when we turned on the bomb run from the Initial Point (IP) to the target was: no one is to do any evasive action; we all were to fly straight and level in order that our mission might be more successful; we all then had the same chance of being hit by the flak. He was both a brave and tough leader.

2nd Mission – Ludwigshaven, Germany: January 7, 1944

This day at 4 a.m. I was awakened with the words, "You're flying with 1st Lt. Inman Jobe in ship number 017." I was again being sent with an experienced crew. Jobe was one of the few original pilots with the 381st Bomb Group. After the two fresh eggs' breakfast, we learned that the target was Ludwigshaven, one of Germany's most important industrial centers. Our target was the I.G. Farben Chemical Works. Although there were plenty of FW190s and ME109s in the air, they were unable to reach us because of the superb fighter cover of Spitfires, P40s and Lightnings. Aside from the bombing, those new P38s covering us near the target was the most outstanding thing about the mission.[6] Bombing results were questionable because of the nine-tenths cloud cover over the target. Naturally there was heavy flak resulting in the loss of one of the Forts of our 381st Bomb Group. We learned later that two crewmen had been killed but the other eight had managed to bail out, becoming Prisoners of War (POWs). For that mission we had been in the air nearly 8 hours.

Before I began flying combat, I wrote home, "These letters don't have much news. It's about all I can think of without giving away any military information. This security is no joke." Finally I was beginning to receive mail. It was heartening to read a letter like this one from Aunt Tilda Landswerk in which she concluded, "Ted, May God be with you and keep his guiding hands over you. That is the prayer from our house".

After that mission I was able to have a couple days off and went to Cambridge, the college town, about 25 miles northwest of our base. I wrote on January 9th, "I was in many of the colleges and saw their chapels, halls and rooms. The most beautiful building is King's College Chapel, which almost compares with some parts of Westminster Abbey in London. I had a very nice room in a hotel and was awakened in the morning with the traditional cup of tea at my bedside. It's great to see some of those old buildings that have stood since before America was even 'discovered' (by Europeans, I should have added!).

3rd Mission – Oschersleben, Germany: January 11, 1944

"Homdrom, you are flying today in ship 895 with Lt. Ridley in squadron lead," was my wake-up call. Now that Gen. Jimmy Doolittle had taken over the 8th Air Force, he began implementing the objective of striking aircraft production plants which were deep into Germany,[7] Oschersleben being only 70 miles from Berlin. Our target was a Focke Wulf fighter assembly plant.

Originally 800 bombers and several hundred fighters were being sent on this strategic mission, but for some reason, possibly the closing in of the weather over England, the raid was cancelled when the bombers were already 30 minutes over the continent. As a result, most of the fleet, including many of the fighters, returned to England. But a much smaller number of Fortresses, including our group, never got the message and proceeded with limited fighter escort to the target. This was suicide – a bad 8th Air Force foul-up! We were alone to battle the FW190s, which came in after us during the entire mission. Waist gunner John Mills from our 535th Squadron wrote this about a nearby bomber that was hit by a German fighter and had to leave the formation: "My heart suddenly goes to my throat and my eyeballs almost pop when suddenly there is a blinding flash as the bomber explodes in a thousand pieces. I feel sick and can't stop my knees from trembling.... A minute ago there had been a 30-ton plane loaded with bombs and a crew of 10 flesh and blood men.... A huge cloud of smoke is all that is left. I saw no chutes come out."[8] A tail gunner from another plane in our squadron, S/Sgt. Wayne Pegg, wrote, "Forts were going down in flames, blowing up and everything. Prestwood's ship broke in half, the ball turret went down separate, no one had a chance."[9] In spite of these attacks, 139 Fortresses managed to bomb the target, but 42 bombers with their crews, eight from our group, were lost. To have 80 men from our base no longer with us that night was devastating. It was a somber few days for all of us. We now knew that there was a long road ahead for those of us who could even hope to survive. Two days later our US Armed Forces newspaper had huge headlines: "Smashing Blow Dealt Nazi Plane Output" and "U.S. aircraft shoot down more than 100 enemy ships in raging dogfight."[10] For the mission our group was awarded the Presidential Distinguished Unit Citation (Appendix A), an award which entitled us to wear the blue ribbon on the right breast. We were given official credit for the destruction of 28 German fighters.[11]

In spite of what had happened, we still sustained a sense of humor – probably a bit questionable. While shaving in the latrine the next morning, I heard a fellow flyer's mirror crash. He remarked, "Oh shucks, seven years of bad luck". I quickly replied, "That's not bad luck. You'll have to live seven years!"

4th Mission – Rouen, France:
January 21, 1944

After my 1st three missions had been with older crews, I was told that for the time being I could fly with Lt. Jim Liddle and our original crew. Initially he had spent time in the hospital in order to clear up some respiratory ailment. Due to the unsuitable weather for visual bombing, we got in very few missions in January. This "milk-run" was welcome after the "massacre" we went through on the 11th. As on Christmas Eve, we tried to locate rocket gun emplacements, but from about 12,000-ft. high and hazy clouds below, we at first could not locate our briefed target. However, after several passes we were finally able to do great damage to the installation. Our Group Commanding Officer, Col. Leber, described the mission as a "bombardier's dream" because there were no fighters or flak.[12]

Even though the winter weather hampered us from flying many missions, we became more and more adjusted to this new life. Because I had sung in the Concordia College A Cappella Choir, I joined some men in a chorus that sang at our Sunday services (for those not on duty, of course). We also had training flights when possible and learned how to become more proficient using the British secret navigational invention, the GEE Box (described in the orientation in the page before my 1st mission), which was installed in our planes. They were not to get into the hands of the Germans. If our plane was going to go down, we had a button to push to blow it up. With weather conditions over England this was a very valuable aid. We could even home in on a runway! The British also had an excellent air-sea rescue system as well as constant radar assistance from the ground to aid "lost" planes wanting a field on which to land. The procedure was for the pilot to circle, calling "Darky" three times on the radio. After being positively identified, he was given the heading and distance to the nearest airfield.

After this mission I had another nice pass, this time to Oxford where the other famous university is. I was keen to compare it with Cambridge. Each university, of course, believes it is the best. Each had certain advantages just as colleges and universities in the U.S. have.

On February 1 it was a pleasant surprise to receive our flying pay for the past 3 months. I wrote to my mother, "I paid $300 for four $100 war bonds, which will come in four to six weeks at home in my name with you as beneficiary." There were some huge poker and other gambling games, which I was happy to ignore. While some won a lot, others were devastated, because a few not only lost everything but also kept borrowing, leaving them with debts to pay the following month or months.

5th Mission – Wilhelmshaven, Germany: February 3, 1944

Although all crews on this mission from Wilhelmshaven to England on February 3 returned to our bases, our crew "sweated out" this one. It was an unusually strong wind, especially at the upper altitudes. Even though we took advantage of this 100-knot tail wind going over the target, we lost an engine that had a direct hit from the heavy flak. In order to avert extra strain on the other three engines, we had to leave the safety of the formation and start homeward on a reduced speed gradual descent. We were in the dangerous position of being a prime target for German fighters, but fortunately we were not attacked. Most likely they were occupied with other near-disabled bombers from other groups. This meant that we had a very low "ground" speed over the North Sea, making less than 100 miles per hour.

When Liddle surprisingly asked me for a heading to Scotland, which he thought was the nearest place to land, he instead was given a heading to our base. After the 1st hour of this slow return into the wind, he asked if I thought we'd make it to Scotland. I replied that I had given the heading to our base. When Jim replied "What!?" I calmly told him that the distance to our base was shorter and that "besides, don't you remember that tonight we have our monthly ice cream party?" This remark immediately did away with the tension of the entire crew during the remaining two hours across the North Sea. All the other crews and ground personnel were relieved when

45

they saw that we had made it back. I had never in my life enjoyed ice cream as much as I did that night! Now we also had the experience of returning alone with a disabled Flying Fortress. I wondered what other experiences I would have on future missions.

6th Mission – Frankfurt, Germany:
February 4, 1944

Again I was awakened to fly with another experienced pilot, Osce Jones (then Captain) leading the squadron. On July 24, 1943, his eleventh mission, his aircraft had been badly damaged, but fortunately he was able to land with his crew in Sweden.[13] After a short stay there he (then 1st Lt.) and his crew were diplomatically repatriated and returned to our base. His southern accent was delightful. Frankfurt had a large marshalling yard surrounded by industries manufacturing war materials. Although we observed enemy fighters, we were protected as our fighters kept engaging them in dogfights. However, the flak was exploding all around us - especially in the target area, but the lead navigator, in not following the flight plan, led us over flak areas which could have been avoided. Nevertheless we were thankful that every bomber returned without any direct hits.

My mother saved all my letters. Although my letters revealed no military information, they were interesting to read when I was writing these "Mission Memories."[14] That night I concluded my self-censored description of life in England with the understatement, "Well, I've had a couple of pretty tough days, so I think I'll go and get some sleep!"

On February 5th, I wrote home that I had recently gone to Cambridge to see the movie "Hers to Hold", starring Diana Durbin. My letter stated, "I had the company of a nice English girl whom I met a couple weeks ago. In such a dangerous life as we had, it meant a great deal to be able to have a little social life with the opposite sex. The English people are extra nice to us and are very hard workers." Just as service men were eager to have such social life, the same was true for the opposite sex. With practically all men in the services, the women were eager to have male company. We had experienced that this was quite true in the U.S. as well.

7th Mission – Nancy, France:
February 6, 1944

Once again I was awakened to fly a combat mission with my original crew, this third time against airfields in France. However, a heavy undercast was encountered, preventing bombing of the principal target. We finally identified another airfield, which we bombed. I recall one serious but humorous incident. Our tail gunner, a full-blooded Hopi Indian, Emery Naha, reported on the intercom "Fighters coming in, 6 o'clock (from the rear)". Our pilot said, "well, shoot them". With his thumb on the intercom button and simultaneously on the 50-caliber machine gun trigger, we heard his slow-speaking voice saying "I am shooting", while we felt the plane vibrating.

One of our planes was so badly damaged that the navigator, bombardier and co-pilot, thinking it was out of control, bailed out. The pilot, Lt. Henry Putek, was greatly assisted by Sgt. Lifford French, who was badly burned but yet was able to extinguish the flames in the flight deck. With the windshield blown out by the explosion, the freeze effects of the windstream made them descend to less cold temperatures. Nevertheless they had a tortuous trip hedgehopping with their crippled plane, finally crash-landing back in England.[15] They were later awarded for their gallantry, French the Distinguished Service Cross and Putek the Silver Star. I was present for the awards ceremony and was indeed proud of them. Besides bringing back the plane, they had risked their lives in order to save the rest of the crew.

Friendly people who were willing to also risk their lives assisted the three who had bailed out over Europe. When they eventually returned to our base, they had many interesting stories to tell of their ordeal.

8th Mission – Frankfurt, Germany: February 11, 1944

I was again awakened to fly with my original crew, this time to Frankfurt marshalling yards. Assembly and flight to the target was quite normal except that I felt that our pilot Jim Liddle was a bit over-aggressive in keeping as close as possible to the next plane. The waist gunner of the nearest bomber wondered if our wing would come in to his window. Admittedly this gave us crew members more protection. Jim was excellent at the controls. Nevertheless, this constant maneuvering took extra fuel due to the continual adjustment and readjustment of throttles and mixture controls. Then, too, as we approached Frankfurt the contrails of previous wings forced the formation to climb higher. This also used up precious fuel.

On our return to the French coast, Jim told the crew that he was afraid our fuel would not hold out until we reached the English coast. He ordered the crew to throw everything heavy, such as guns, ammunition, flak suits, etc. into the sea. Air Sea Rescue was called as we prepared to ditch in the cold North Sea. As we approached the White Cliffs of Dover, he saw what appeared to be a beautiful green meadow where sheep were grazing, so he decided to make a go for it.

What Jim hadn't seen from the distance at that low altitude was the barbed wire entanglement, electric highline wire and eight-foot wide ditch across the meadow. Nevertheless in we went with wheels up to crash-land. The rear part of the plane barely cleared the barbed wire entanglement, the high tail barely got under the highline wire, but just beyond was this ditch. The engines caught in that and the plane's waist buckled upward as we came to a jarring halt. Although we all survived, our ball turret gunner Jack Burke had two cracked ribs. (As he was getting near the end of his tour, which was still limited to 25 missions, he didn't report his injury, because he wanted to finish quickly. When he was to be sent for another tour of combat, he failed his physical exam because of that injury.)[16] After a military truck ride to the next village to make a telephone call and to the nearest airfield, a Flying Fortress from our base picked us up.

Now we had had the experience of a crash-landing also. I wondered what other experiences we would have on future missions. Although it would have been good to land at an airfield, at least we were thankful not to have ditched in the cold North Sea. Many who ditched on previous recent missions simply didn't survive.

As the plane was a write-off from flying again, I removed a dinghy knife, which could float in water and was designed not to pierce the inflatable life raft. I still have this unique memento from that crash-landing. All I wrote the next day to my mother was "There's not much to tell you, but we have plenty of excitement all the time. I'm beginning to wonder if I could settle down to a quiet life of teaching again." I also thanked her for another box of candy, saying, "What you send surely doesn't last long." Actually, we who were in the military and especially we who were flying, had a much better diet than the ordinary civilians on the strict war-time food rationing.

As I learned on another pass to London, even restaurants had a scarcity of many food items. However, their menus, especially in what I would call a swanky place, attempted to show high class. When I was in London, I thought I would visit one of those. The waiters, mostly French I believe, were dressed in formal attire. Their every action, including sitting me at the table, handing me the menu, responding to questions about the possible choices and bringing each course, came with a "Thank you", which sounded like "hank yo". Yet in reply to my question about what kind of soup with a French name was on the menu, he replied, "It's very nice thin soup, 'hank yo'". When it came with a "hank yo", I was certain that it was nothing but a bouillon cube in hot water. The veal patty must have had at least 90% corn meal. When I asked about another French name, I was told that it was cabbage. On the base we had Brussels sprouts day in and day out until we were all very tired of it. Consequently I enthusiastically ordered the cabbage. When it came on a nice dish with a "hank yo", what could it really be but Brussels sprouts!? These waiters had high tips added to the accounts and I learned that those jobs are so well protected by the waiters that they will sell their positions when they resign or retire. Needless to say, I received my lesson to avoid such a swanky place in the future. It was much safer to settle for good old fish and chips at an ordinary restaurant, tearoom or pub.

On that pass I also saw the 375 feet high St. Paul's Cathedral, which I had missed on the previous visit. At a height of 100 feet is the Whispering Gallery, which is over one hundred feet across. A person on one side of the dome speaking practically in a whisper was heard on the other side. Because of some German bomb damage, we could only ascend 375 of the 625 steps, but even at that height we could see the whole city of London. Having had a major in history in college, I felt I was really privileged to visit these influential places that I had only read about previously. Overseas travel for US students at that time was simply out of the question. I guess it was at least some compensation for the dangerous life we were leading. On that pass Joe Harapat from my home town and I met on the streets of London! I don't recall what branch of the service he was serving. We both were thrilled at this remarkable coincidence.

During this longer period between my 8th and 9th missions I was awakened to fly with my original crew once again. Everything went well with our usual preparations, take-off and joining the formation into Germany. However, over the continent Jim said he was aborting due to some faulty instrument. Realizing the danger of flying alone over enemy territory, he saw a group of B-26s returning from their earlier mission and increased our speed by about 20 miles per hour to join them.

Back over England Jim told us he wanted to visit a fighter pilot friend on the way. With our heavy plane, still with its bomb load and much fuel, he landed on this grass field covered by a metal grid. This was the roughest landing I had ever experienced. After lunch there we again bounced tremendously to get airborne. To top it off, he then came back low over the airfield and "buzzed" the tower. When we finally got back to our base, I was wondering if it would have been safer flying the mission! What was worst was that even though we had been over the continent we did not, of course, get credit for a mission. Furthermore, an abortion without a very good reason was frowned upon by our superiors.

Contrails made by formation of Fortresses at high altitude
US Air Force photo, reprinted with permission

9th Mission – Leipzig, Germany:
February 20, 1944

After the past two missions with my original crew, I was designated to fly this mission with Lt. Rowland Evans, who had earned his Ph.D. and was a philosophy professor at Williams College in Massachusetts. Believing strongly in democratic causes, he had enlisted. Apparently his navigator was for some reason unable to fly that day, so I was awakened to fly with him and his crew.

The destruction of the Luftwaffe on the ground or in the air continued to be a top priority with Generals Spaatz and Doolittle.[17] Since most aircraft plants lay beyond the immediate escort cover, bomber losses of up to 20% were allowed.[18] In other words, we were expendable! However, on this deep mission into Germany, our fighter escort rendezvous at all points was such that the enemy aircraft were largely kept at bay. Also, of the 1,003 bombers out that day attacking other aircraft factories in two other areas, the Luftwaffe had to spread out its defenses. Good bombing results were reported at all three targets, making this one of the most successful raids of the 8th Air Force. It had been a long strenuous day, but I merely wrote in my letter home, " I'm awfully sleepy, so I think I'll hit the sack."

Tragic note: 2 days later, on February 22, this outstanding man, Lt. Rowland Evans, flew on a mission to Bunde, Germany. Six bombers from our 381st Bomb Group were shot down. Evans flew that mission as co-pilot with Lt. Lee Smith as pilot.[19] When I heard that they went down in flames, I remembered a couple of lines of the Army Air Corps song: "We live in fame or go down in flame." None of us who were still alive felt as though he was still living in fame. I felt deep mental anguish for those with whom I had just flown 2 days previously. At times like that a drink or so at the Officers' Club and talking with a few of my colleagues helped minimize the stress. In my prayer before going to sleep that night I knew that my life was indeed in his hands and that I could suffer the same fate the next day or on any future mission.

10th Mission – Schweinfurt, Germany: February 24, 1944

When I was awakened to once again fly with Liddle and our original crew, I wondered what was in store for us this day. We were pretty apprehensive when we learned that out target would be the ball bearing factories at Schweinfurt, where former raids there had resulted in such great losses as 60 bombers. However, the 8th Air Force had grown in size and strength. Also, what was especially welcome was that groups of long-range fighters had been established in England.

Gen. Eaker and his staff were determined to use every means to cripple Germany by attacking the basic supplies for waging war. Simultaneously, attacks on oil refineries, bridges, railroad marshalling yards, supply trains, submarine pens and aircraft factories that week divided the Luftwaffe's defenses. Our Group had good bombing results, but I seem to recall that it was on this mission that we had a new experience.

We had not yet had the experience of weather closing in on our return to our base in England. Starting from the continent and over the North Sea, we could no longer fly in formation. To avoid collisions, three planes descended simultaneously. The center bomber continued the same compass heading while the right plane initially flew a bit to the right and the left one a bit to the left before resuming their original heading down, until they leveled off just when they saw the water. This was followed by successive elements of three until all bombers were down through the "soup".

As we descended, I carefully watched the altimeter, which I had set correctly before take-off. When I saw the needle at 200 ft., 100 ft., 50 ft., and then going below zero without my seeing the water, I called to the pilot, "What is this, a submarine?" Just then, at about minus 50 ft., we saw the water and leveled off. What had happened was that the weather change made the air pressure change, which affected the setting on our altimeters.

But our ordeal was not yet over. How could we see the English coast to ascend from sea level soon enough with such poor visibility? Fortunately we did, barely missing another Fortress. Furthermore, at that low altitude and poor visibility I could not identify at which point we entered Britain. We then used the marvelous English aid called "Darky". We were then given a heading and distance to the nearest airfield.

We were all dead tired but greatly relieved when we piled out of the plane. As we observed our plane, we were horrified to see a huge head-sized hole just where the tail gunner's head was during flight. We asked our barrel-chested Indian Naha what had happened. He said that the approaching German fighters' 20 mm shell had exploded there just when he was reaching back for more ammunition. Hearing that, we slap-happy fliers just roared with laughter. Fighters and flak had left about 1,000 holes in our plane but the weather had attempted to add insult to injury. Our tail gunner found that night that his shirt stuck to his back. It had been hit by bits of the exploding shell. We certainly had kept our guardian angels busy that day. That night I wondered what other close calls I could have and still survive. Yet I dared pray for the Lord's protection if it was his will that I did come through this ordeal.

During the past couple of months certain portions of the Bible, such as Psalm 91 became very personal and comforting to me: "You will not fear the terror of the night, or the arrow that flies by day, or the destruction that wastes at noonday. A thousand may fall at your side, ten thousand at your right hand, but it will not come near you." Not that this made me feel invincible, but some of the phrases described what I had experienced thus far.

Incidentally, this was my last mission with my original crew. I had flown half of my ten missions with other crews. Having proven that I was reliable under stress, I was apparently reserved for missions where lead crews required a responsible and experienced navigator.

During this week, February 19-25, which included these two missions in which I had flown; the RAF put 2,300 bombers over Germany at night and the American Air Force 3,800 during daytime. Desperately seeking to fend off this particular service of assaults, the Luftwaffe lost 450 planes – a rate which it could not long sustain."[20]

11th Mission – Frankfurt, Germany: March 2, 1944

After nearly a week the weather opened up somewhat. This time I was told I was flying with Lt. Charles Stang to Frankfurt. Again I was pleased to be navigating for a crew with more missions than I had. The target was the Alfred Ternes aircraft component factory. There were a few fighters and moderate inaccurate flak. Consequently we achieved what we were expected to do.

Our Group Chaplain James Good Brown had wanted to see what his men went through in combat and, with difficulty obtaining approval, flew with our group. This was the first of his five "officially unapproved" missions. He wrote much about his reactions to the experience.[21] The only crew that did not return from that mission was that of 1st Lt. Eugene Schultz, but at least eight parachutes were seen as the bomber went down. Chaplain Brown mentioned that Schultz and he had grown up together in their hometown in Pennsylvania. Consequently, he was very concerned about what happened to him.

On the mission Chaplain Brown started in the nose of the bomber with the bombardier and navigator, visiting with each person in his position and working his way back to the tail gunner. He concluded the story of his mission by writing, "I know this: when I got out of the plane, I was a changed person. I now knew firsthand how all my fliers feel when they step out of the plane on their return from combat and breathe that good fresh air, bequeathed to them by Divine Nature."[22]

Old B-17-F NOSE interior: Bombardier up front, Navigator's desk at left behind him

12th Mission – Oldenburg, Germany: March 3, 1944

On this day I again flew with a different crew, this time with another very experienced pilot, 1st Lt. George McIntosh. He had been co-pilot for Osce Jones (then 1st Lt.) on a mission to Norway on July 24, 1943, when their damaged plane was able to land in Sweden.[23] When he was repatriated and returned to our base at Ridgewell, he was given a crew of his own. However, on a mission on February 21, 1944, he had brought home his plane with a burned nose section and gaping bomb bay doors as well as having his navigator and co-pilot bail out over Europe. They had thought the plane would explode or certainly crash. For that brave struggle he was awarded the Distinguished Flying Cross.

He was to have the deputy Group lead this time with me assigned as the navigator to take Lt. Piekerski's place. The mission went as briefed up to and beyond the enemy coast, but because of increasing cloud formations, we were forced to fly up to 28,000 feet. This resulted in a mid-air collision with the loss of one of our bombers and crew. It became utter chaos to try to stay in formation. After much confusion, the bombing of the primary target was abandoned. Often the weather determined where we bombed; we then struck the secondary target, Wilhelmshaven, a very important port in northern Germany.

From England it was very difficult to predict what the weather would be over Europe and even what the conditions would be like when we returned from a mission. Consequently some missions had to be aborted even after we were over the continent. Nevertheless, the 8th Air Force was under pressure to attack as much of the Nazi military production as possible in order to lessen the losses in the predicted invasion. Sometimes we took off in questionable weather only to find favorable bombing conditions in German-held territory. Thus we became more conditioned for the early wake-up call for a mission.

13th Mission – Duesseldorf, Germany: March 4, 1944

For the third day in a row I was awakened for a mission and for the second time in a row I flew with 1st Lt. McIntosh. This time we flew deputy Wing lead. By now there was a strong determination on the part of the Air Force leadership to bomb Berlin.[24] Again the weather was unfavorable for flying in formation. Our final Division assembly did not materialize as planned. One combat wing aborted the mission at the enemy coast, while the rest of us continued. Cloud formations became worse. It was then decided to abandon the attempt to reach the primary target. Our Group's alternate target of Duesseldorf, where much war-producing industry was located, was then bombed. Due to heavy flak, our Group lost one Fortress with its 10-member crew. However, in anticipation of longer missions, we became more worried about what losses longer missions would incur if our target should be Berlin. That symbolized the place where Hitler would use every weapon he could throw up at us. "Latrine rumors" were increasingly evolving that any mission would soon be the "Big B."

Fortresses in moderate flak
US Air Force photo, reprinted with permission

14th Mission – BERLIN:
March 6, 1944

As the curtains were pulled aside in the briefing room, the Intelligence Officer said, "You are going to Berlin." As this was a massive strike of nearly 700 bombers[25], we were placed in almost any formation that needed completion. I flew in the low Squadron of the high Group with another experienced pilot, Lt. Tom Honahan, a New Yorker with whom I hadn't flown before. Several bombers from the 91st Bomb Group were to join us in order to complete the Wing formation. One crewman was heard to remark after the briefing, "The queues to the toilet are three times as long today." This was after all the "Big B", which we all feared.

As I so vividly recall, we were flying along to our destination when about 36 ME109s came head-on through our low squadron, known as "coffin corner". All of us on the crew who had a gun or guns were firing at those German fighters. I had a gun at each side window. As I followed one, simultaneously firing my right 50-caliber machine gun, I saw a huge explosion. It was the ME 109 but also a nearby bomber. My knees were shaking as I feared that I might have caused it.

(Here I must make an aside. From early youth I had had what I felt was a call to become a minister. Being a shy person, I never mentioned this to anyone. As no one of my ancestors had ever been in the ministry, I felt it was too high a calling for me and resisted it.)

After this pass, as I recall, of the enemy fighters shooting down or damaging three of the six bombers in our squadron formation, I breathed a prayer, "Lord, if you see me through this, I'll do what you want me to do." As the ME109s came through the remaining three B-17s of our formation, they shot down the one on our right and one on our left. I learned later that one of the five planes that I thought had been shot down was the one flown by Lt. Tyson. His navigator, John Howland, wrote in his book that he and the bombardier had had close calls. The window by the navigator's desk had been pulverized – showering them with bits of plexiglass.[26] That crew left our Squadron shortly thereafter to go to Pathfinder School. They were very good crew members and would later assist our Group when cloudy conditions were possible at the target area. After that Honahan told me that he just wanted to hide and tagged on to another squadron above us.[27] Although I personally believed that my prayer had been answered, I at the same time felt very sorrowful for those who had gone down. We all hoped that most of them would become POWs.

This first daylight mission to Berlin lost 69 bombers. Each side lost about 100 fighters as well. Nevertheless the European Theatre of Operations High Command considered this satisfactory, because while the US production and training programs could quite rapidly replace these airplanes and crews, the Germans could not.

At the usual interrogation after we returned, I at least was relieved to know that the German fighter I had been firing at had crashed into the B-17 and both had exploded. We had assumed that our fire had hit the ME109 pilot. Even though this attack took only a few seconds, it was a horrible thing to remember knowing that ten of our men and the German pilot at that moment lost their lives! Our crew was credited with destroying 4 fighters, so I might have at least assisted in destroying the one I was firing at.

The next day as usual I carefully avoided giving away military secrets, merely writing to my mother, "We surely have had a tough week." Later, in the midst of another paragraph, I wrote, "Rest assured your prayers are being answered when you pray for my safety." It's hard to imagine how one could endure the stress of four such missions in five days! We had rapidly become seasoned combat veterans through many narrow escapes and experiences.

We had much to talk about over our food and drinks at the Officers Club that evening. One officer drew laughs as he paraphrased what he imagined our new 8th Air Force CO Gen. Jimmy Doolittle (since Jan. 1) could have said, "I bombed Tokyo, I bombed Rome, YOU bomb Berlin!" Anyway such a mixture of talking and laughing with the fellows helped a lot to ease the tension. And it was very tense! After all, one or more of us socializing that evening could be among the missing or killed the very next mission. More than ever I felt I was in the Lord's hand.

15th Mission – Berlin:
March 8, 1944

Can you imagine what I could be thinking when again we were flying to the "Big B"? I felt I couldn't possibly survive another, but as always on take-off I breathed "Lord, I'm in your hands." I was to fly with still another experienced pilot, this time with Lt. Thomas Sellers.

In his book, Ron MacKay tells about Sellers' grim experience on a mission to Bremen on October 8, 1943: "The incident most indelibly imprinted on the minds of the returning crewmen's minds was what happened to Lt. Hal Minerich... Under fighter attack the B-17 took a burst which ripped off the nose canopy and penetrated the windscreen. Minerich was decapitated and blood pumping from his body sprayed and instantly froze into a slick all over the cockpit. Co-pilot Lt. Thomas Sellers was wounded by the exploding shells but with assistance from T/Sgt. Miller made it home with TINKERTOY ground looping on landing. Sellers was later awarded the Distinguished Service Cross, one of only two won by 381st BG personnel."[28]

I was very impressed to hear about this display of loyalty and courage. Though he was wounded, he most likely could have bailed out. But by mustering all his strength and skill, he was able to bring his pilot back for burial, save the airplane and be assured of the safety of the rest of his crew.

This mission to Berlin could not have been a better morale booster. With good weather we could assemble as scheduled, arrive at the continent on time, pick up groups of escort fighters at each rendezvous point and consequently not be attacked by very many enemy fighters. As we neared the Erkner ball bearing works, we were able to bomb visually. Although the flak was moderate, it wasn't all that accurate. What a difference from the first raid only two days earlier when we lost 69 bombers! On this long mission deep into Germany, 37 bombers were lost – but only one from our Group. Finally the war against the Luftwaffe was bearing results. Although we had invaded the airspace over the German capital with fewer losses, we couldn't become over-confident. The Allies had not yet invaded Europe!

I must have decided to take a chance to give my mother and sister at least confirmation that I was flying combat. On March 12, 1944, I wrote, "I'll send you a clipping of the 1st daylight Berlin raid of March 6th." The newspaper article was, "Told by men who were there." Among the quotes from a dozen flyers was this one from Lt. Col. R. Kuttie, a wing leader: " We were under fighter attack for nearly 5 hours. The assaults were bold and vicious, coming from every conceivable position."[29]

I believe the censors of our mail allowed information like that to go through. After all, the news was in all the newspapers and on radio. We who were officers not only censored the enlisted men's letters but also our own. However, the intelligence officers could spot check our work. Consequently we had to be rather strict on all our censoring, lest we be severely reprimanded and perhaps demoted. It was interesting to hear later from our ball-turret gunner about censoring. He said, "I always came with my letters to Ted, because he would tell me where I had misspelled words. He was my mentor while O'Phelan was my drinking buddy." However, after five missions in seven days, I felt I had the duty to give my relatives a little hint that I was living quite a dangerous life.

I also happily grabbed the opportunity for a much-needed break to once again visit London. Arriving at the train station that morning, I phoned Regents Street Hotel, which was situated in the busy movie theater area, for a room. When I heard that it was fully booked, I told my friend Patrick O'Phelan that we'd better take the room that was offered by the station. While we were near Piccadilly Circus eating lunch in what I recall was a Chinese restaurant, we decided not to observe the air raid warning nor to follow the crowd to a bomb shelter. After all, we were close to explosions of various kinds practically every mission. We flyers haughtily called those fleeing "paddle feet." Moments later a huge explosion somewhere near even caused ceiling plaster to fall on our food. I quite calmly told Pat, "Hmm, close, wasn't it?" Outdoors, glass from department store windows lay on the sidewalk. The very hotel that we had called that morning for a booking had been hit by a V-2 buzz bomb. We later learned that only two, both cleaning ladies, had been killed, because the hotel guests were out for lunch or sightseeing. Could one say that I was once again miraculously spared? (In this case, though, I suppose I could be guilty of foolhardily keeping my guardian angel working overtime!)

16th Mission – Mannheim, Germany: March 20, 1944

When I was assigned to fly with Lt. Henry Putek, I was pleased because he was one of the best pilots in our squadron. I already mentioned that on my 7th mission his plane was so badly damaged that part of the crew, including the navigator, Lt. Conrad Blalok, believing that the Fortress could not possibly continue flying much longer, had bailed out over the continent. As the 2nd most experienced navigator left in the squadron, I was assigned for the time being to fill the role of his missing crew member. Putek and I became very good friends.

As the wind had been predicted to be from the north at about 100 knots at approximately 25,000 ft., we were carried quickly to the continent; nevertheless the contrails from the bombers were very heavy, forming a cloud after each wing formation of 54 bombers. Because each succeeding wing formation had to climb higher, nearly up to 30,000 ft., by the time we arrived nearer the target, our heavy Fortresses struggled, finding ourselves in these bomber-made clouds. As we dropped our bombs over the target, we were horrified to see another formation flying right through our group, causing at least two bombers to collide near us. It was horrible to observe one breaking up in about six pieces! Instantly our formation was broken up, leaving us all alone. Putek asked me for the heading and, allowing for the strong north wind, I gave him a heading of west north west (about 300 degrees). When the pilot saw another formation flying in somewhat the same direction, he decided it would be safer joining them, especially because they were led by a Pathfinder ship, which could see through the clouds. When I saw that we all were flying at a heading of 270 degrees, I figured that the predicted wind must have changed. After all they had the Pathfinder plane. When we had been flying "blindly" with them for about half an hour, I could finally see ground clearly below. I tried to pick out where we were, but unfortunately we had only been issued strip maps for our planned route.

The only extra possible help that I remembered I had in my briefcase was a small map of Europe. I had only used this to mark in red wherever I had observed flak on previous missions. Hence I called it my "flak map". About all it showed, besides the red marks I had made, was the coastline and rivers. As we flew on another half hour or so without identifying where we were, I noticed that we had had for some time below us a river flowing practically due west. On the flak map, there was only one flowing in that direction in all of France. That was the Loire River.

I called the pilot, telling him that I had just discovered where we were and that we would have to fly almost due north by now if we wanted to get back to England. As he saw a large body of water (the Bay of Biscay) way ahead, he felt it was safer to stick with the formation and see what they would do. To our amazement they flew straight on; consequently, near St. Nazaire. Putek agreed to take my heading. At least a dozen planes, seeing us leaving the formation, began following us. What a joy it was for us after going north for over an hour against the strong wind to see England ahead. My GEE Box became operative, confirming my inference. After the huge detour from the planned route, we thought our pilot would want to land at the first possible airfield. However, he informed us that there still was some fuel. When we finally landed at our base, our Group Commander reprimanded Putek for landing earlier and not informing them. "I notified Division Headquarters an hour ago that you were Missing in Action!" He was really shocked when he learned that we had not landed and that we had been in the air eleven and a half hours! Then he congratulated us and showed that he was extremely grateful that we had returned. My little flak map had saved our lives and many others.

The next day we learned that a few of the bombers from the group that we had followed had landed in Spain. However, all the others except those that had followed us, had disappeared. It became known as the worst navigation error in ETO history. In my case it was just the opposite; it was up until then my best job of navigating.

Nevertheless, I was saddened to hear that Lt. McIntosh, with whom I had flown two missions, had not returned from that raid. Ron MacKay reported the following about McIntosh's final mission over Europe: "Now on his 14th mission he was startled to find that, when he broke cloud cover he was over what turned out to be the Normandy coast rather than the briefed cross-point at the Pas de Calais. Already suffering engine failure on one engine of his Fortress, he now suffered similar failures in two of the remaining engines, leaving him with no choice but to ditch just off the coast. Only one dinghy could be inflated into which eight men scrambled, leaving McIntosh and Sgt. Eugene Copp to cling onto the raft liners. Fortunately a French boat picked them up, saving them from the deadly numbing channel waters to begin the long haul to a POW camp."[30] We were happy to hear that he, who had had several narrow escapes in his combat career, and the crew were POWs.

A group of Flying Fortresses over Germany
US Air Force photo, reprinted with permission

Homdrom at his navigation desk in the bomber's nose

17th Mission – Frankfurt, Germany:
March 24, 1944

With pilot Putek again, we were briefed to bomb the primary target, Schweinfurt. As we ascended through the billowing clouds, two of our bombers crashed into each other. It was a sad day for our Group because one plane crashed shortly after take-off, killing all ten men. Three Flying Fortresses and 30 men were lost and not one was due to enemy action! Flying in such weather conditions became one of our greatest fears. If it were not for the weather, the bomber crews would have gone on to bomb the target no matter how many planes would have been shot down on the way. At least there would have been the satisfaction for those returning that they did all they could in attempting to cripple the German war effort.

As we could not fly very well in formation that day, most of us bombed Frankfurt, the secondary target. Consequently some damage had been done to the German war production, but at what a cost! We were deeply saddened by the loss of many men. Chaplain Brown wrote several pages on the horrible crash and explosion and also about the reaction of us who returned. "I shall not forget the look on the men's faces when they came into the interrogation room. The lines in their faces showed more clearly. Eyes were strained. Their talk was rapid and serious. They looked as though they had lived in hell. They were disgusted. They were peeved at someone, they knew not whom. They thought someone higher up had not done his job;

he had not read the weather properly. The flyers cannot conquer the cosmic forces."[31]

18th Mission – Calais, France:
March 26, 1944

After a day's very welcome break, this short flight across the English Channel was another attempt to bomb the German V-bomb launching sites. I flew with Lt. Putek, leading one of the squadron's formations of six Flying Fortresses. No attempt was made to assemble as combat wings and, interestingly enough, the bombing was done by squadrons because of at least four of the scattered sites plotted by Intelligence. We also returned to England without forming into group formations. Although many planes from our 381st were damaged, all returned safely. The 306th Group was not so fortunate, having 26 of its 29 planes hit; 17 of them were seriously damaged and two crash-landed back in England and had to be salvaged.[32]

Having had the experience of the power of the latest V-2 bombs, as I mentioned in my 15th mission, I was pleased that we had the opportunity to attack these launching sites on the "rocket coast".

19th Mission – St. Jean de Angely, France: March 27, 1944

It seems that the 8th Air Force had learned that there were poor bombing results and many unnecessary losses of bombers and crews when weather was bad. Better weather on the 27th March meant more flying. 290 bombers were dispatched to bomb airports in France.[33] My flight with Lt. Putek was one of the few without any memorable incidents. I recall having a feeling of satisfaction to have had a part in badly damaging our target as well as to chalk up another mission that we called "milk-runs" (those not far into France). At that time a tour consisted of 25 missions. I wondered if the number would remain at that figure, and, if so, I would need only six more!

20th Mission – Reims, France:
March 28, 1944

Flying with Lt. Putek in the squadron lead position, we were sent to bomb more airfields in France. The Allied High Command wanted to prevent Germany from establishing air bases closer to the French coastline, where it was assumed the Allies would invade. Also, these bases, if established, would allow fighters to attack the bombing raids more quickly.

Our 381st Bomb Group had moderate but accurate flak at Reims. Lt. Liddle and my original crew, with whom I had flown five missions, were also on that mission. On the way out, the No. 3 engine caught fire and Liddle aborted. As altitude was decreased, the fire (fed by the increased oxygen level) gained in intensity. When they reached the Kent area in England, he gave the bailout order. All ten, including the tough little tail gunner, Sgt. Emory Y. Naha, the full-blooded Hopi Indian, exited safely. Lt. Joe Scott, who took my place as navigator on the crew, "used initiative when we put up at the local hotel; with no US currency on hand, he persuaded the manager to accept his French escape-kit money."[34]

Many years later our ball turret-gunner, S/Sgt. John Burke, received an appeal from someone in England trying to trace just how this bomber had come down. After the rest of the crew had bailed out and before he jumped, Liddle had, as he said, set the autopilot for the plane to fly out into the North Sea. Whatever happened is a mystery as to whether the autopilot was faulty – or whether the plane simply crashed. This local resident wrote to Burke, "the ship nearly wiped out my father's dairy and the local village." The field was called "Fortress Field."[35] By being with another crew, I was happy to have evaded that experience.

On the same mission, the Fortress named WHODAT met with a far worse catastrophe. Moments after dropping its bombs, the tail section was hit by two flak bursts. Ron MacKay describes the calamity as follows: "The effect was to practically sever the tail, which was left hanging by mere shards of metal. This hit also killed the waist and tail gunners. With the elevators jammed in the up position and with severed rudder cables, Lt. Dan C. Henry and Lt. Crisler somehow pulled their battered B-17 out of the dive and headed for home with eight P-38s as escort. Sgt. Quaresma managed to lash enough of the rudder cables together to provide some control for the pilots.... When Ridgewell was reached, the other five crewmen jumped (attempts to land being too risky). Henry and Crisler then took their gallant cripple out over the Essex coast where they jumped, leaving WHODAT to fall harmlessly into the sea."[36]

21st Mission – Brunswick, Germany: March 29, 1944

On this mission with Lt. Putek, we flew the High Group lead position. Interestingly enough the future lead pilot in the squadron, Capt. Charles Enos, flew with us as Group leader sitting in the co-pilot's seat. I felt fortunate to fly with these two outstanding pilots. Due to some clouds at the primary target, we bombed the secondary objective, Brunswick, a city with many strategic industrial plants. Although the 8th Air Force lost eight aircraft out of the 236 planes dispatched, all from our 381st Bomb Group returned.[37] However, our CO, then major Halsey, flying deputy Wing lead, had to leave the formation after his plane's engine was hit. Fortunately P51s saw his dilemma and escorted his plane and crew back to Ridgewell base.

March had been a very important month because the weather had been reasonably tolerable most of the time. During that period I had completed eleven missions with five different crews. As this was my fourth day in a row flying combat, I was really eager for a break. That night my letter home merely stated, "As usual I don't have much news" – certainly an understatement!

Mostly on our minds was what lay ahead in the spring and summer. When and where would the invasion across the Channel be made? England was abuzz with rumors, because the evidence of a monstrous build-up was everywhere. Anyway, we flyers would do all we could to weaken Germany's military might whenever and wherever we were sent.

22nd Mission – Brussels, Belgium: April 10, 1944

Starting in April 1944 the Strategic Bomber Command was given over to General Eisenhower, who wanted to channel most of the Allied war efforts in preparation for the invasion of Europe.[38] For the 7th mission in a row, I was to fly with Lt. Henry Putek, but because I had been appointed Squadron Navigator, this was my final mission with him and his fine crew. From now on I was listed as navigator with the lead crew and would be leading group or wing formations. This, of course, meant more responsibility. A group consisted of 18 bombers with 180 men - a wing formation had 54 Fortresses and 540 men. This promotion also meant that I would not complete my tour as quickly as it seemed, because our squadron led wing formations only about every eighth mission.

This short mission to bomb the airfield near Brussels was to prevent Germany from establishing an airbase there, more a tactical than a strategic raid. Our Group was happy to get such a "milk-run" without any losses.

Incidentally, the day before, which was Easter Sunday, I was on a long mission with a target in Poland. We had been in the air for about 4 hours flying over northern Europe when we received word that the mission was cancelled. Naturally we were not given credit for a mission. As we headed back to England, I remarked on the intercom. "Too bad, we missed Easter service at the chapel." The ball turret gunner came back with, "Well, I prayed much more up here than I would have at church!" Apparently it's not just in foxholes where there are no atheists.

"The Board" in Squadron Operator's office.
Lead crew on top. If a crew fails to return, their
names are erased and a new crew is written in
chalk in its place

23rd Mission – Cottbus, Germany: April 11, 1944

My pilot on that first-ever mission to Cottbus was our squadron lead pilot Capt. Charles Enos. Osce V. Jones (now Major), with whom I had flown my 6th mission after his return from Sweden, was our Low Group leader, occupying the co-pilot seat.

In the briefing on April 11, 1944, we were told that our primary target was Cottbus, where Germany was producing the first jet fighters. It was a high priority target for our air war. I, as Squadron Navigator, with most of the crew of Major Jones, was to lead this Low Group of the Wing. As the huge 54-bomber formation approached the target, there was about a six-tenths cloud cover, giving the Wing lead navigator and bombardier difficulty to visually bomb the jet factory buildings. Hence a 360-degree turn taking about six minutes was made; again the lead bombardier could not identify the target through the holes in the clouds.

But as we approached the general area, the bombardier in our plane, 1st Lt. Eugene Arning, suddenly shouted on the intercom, "Hey, Major, I see the target – 9 o'clock, should we bomb it?" Jones immediately replied, "OK, let's bomb it". With a sharp left-hand turn we had the other 17 planes of our group, which were naturally caught off guard by that unprecedented maneuver, make quite a scattered formation. The other 36 bombers abandoned the efforts to bomb Cottbus and flew on. Within a minute Arning called "OK, bombs away!" The next moment I heard

"OK, Navigator, what's our heading?" This new situation for me, apart from our flight plan, required an instant reply, so I immediately gave the Major a northerly heading with the hope that we could rejoin the rest of the Wing as they came off bombing the secondary target, Stetin. Soon we saw them but cautiously stayed off to their left. By then as we flew northward the clouds below all but disappeared. What a show we saw as the lead and high Groups went through the anti-aircraft flak and bombed their target. When I observed the exploding bombs blanketing the target area, I noticed that the flashes from the flak guns in that area ceased to fire. I assumed that the gunners had either been killed or had fled to some shelter at the last moment.

After such an unheard of departure from the large formation so deep into Germany, we were very relieved to rejoin the rest of the formation as we headed out over the Baltic Sea. As we turned west I noticed that we were close to Sweden and turned on the Swedish radio. Then it was over Denmark on our way back to our base. For that mission we were in the air for 11 hours. What a Cooke's tour of Europe?!

About a month later, at an awards ceremony at our base, I recall our CO announcing something like the following: It has been confirmed by aerial photography that on April 11, 1944, 18 bombers from the 381st Bomb Group broke off from the wing formation, hitting all of the buildings at the Cottbus jet factory, which the entire formation was to attack. Consequently, the members of that Group are awarded the Presidential Citation. (There were also comments about the courage, coolness and skill of the flyers). We were presented with a small blue ribbon with a gold border to wear on the left side of our blouse or shirt. Unfortunately we were not given copies of the citation.

Towards the end of the war, bombing crews reported an occasional jet fighter, but it is believed that our Cottbus mission greatly retarded the production of the much faster plane and made it possible for the 8th Air Force to complete its task with fewer losses.

Two days later, on April 13th, on a mission to the ball bearing works at Schweinfurt, one of the crews in our squadron was missing in action. The pilot was Lt. James Mullane. However, what I felt most sad about was that my original crew bombardier, Patrick O'Phelan from St. Paul, Minnesota, also went down. He was known as a "toggelier" on that mission, keeping the navigator's log as well as being able to fill the role of bombardier. We were relieved to hear that all personnel jumped and became POWs.

I recall an incident in the barracks before Pat went down. As we occupants were sharing the latest of what we experienced, we had an unexpected visit from our Squadron CO, Major Halsey. All of a sudden Pat just burst into tears saying, "Major, I just can't stand this (his descriptive adjective left off) flak any more." Maybe his status to POW was a blessing in disguise!

About the time that Pat went down, I received a St. Paul Dispatch clipping from home about an interview that Staff Correspondent Al Crocker had had with O'Phelan in London. Pat at one time was an office boy on the paper, but had joined the Air Force shortly after Pearl Harbor. Crocker wrote: "A half dozen missions over the continent does something for a youngster. The sparkling wings and snappy uniform lose much of their glamour and come to represent a hard, dangerous job to be carried out slowly, painstakingly and perseveringly until a tour of duty is completed.... Lt. O'Phelan didn't have to tell me his entire story; much of it was apparent from the way he told it and more from other things that we talked about. He told me how good the other members of his crew were – not about himself but about Lt. Theodore Homdrom of Erskine, Minn., his navigator, and some of the crew of gunners."[39] I wrote home thinking of the clipping, merely saying, "He went down, but we're pretty sure he's OK. I was made Squadron Navigator, so I don't fly combat missions very often now. It's a lot of responsibility when I do, though."

Added later: over a year later, in August 1945, after my return to civilian life, I received a call from Pat saying he had returned from the POW camp. What a wonderful reunion we had for a couple of days reminiscing about our experiences. Over 50 years later I met Pat's brother, Dr. Harvey O'Phalen, an orthopedic surgeon. He told me that my letter to his mother had been such a help - instead of being Missing in Action she now knew that he was alive as a POW.

On the 28th of April, I was told that I was flying again with Major Jones. After breakfast, briefing to St. Averd, France, preparing my flight plan and arriving at the ship waiting with the crew for take-off, the Group Navigator, Major Jim Delano, came out to the plane telling me, "Ted, we've decided to save you for longer missions like Berlin; Guertin will fly today." I must admit that I was pretty disgruntled that day, having missed out on such a "milk-run." I had also eagerly anticipated flying again with Major Jones, whom I admired, and Bombardier Gene Arning. We had become very good friends, appreciating each others' skills especially in unexpected circumstances. He was very out-going and was loved by the crew. As usual we waited on the flight line for the return of the bombers, but we noticed how somber the men looked. We were then told that the lead plane, in which I would have been flying with Major Jones, received a direct hit over the target. According to a report by a gunner on another B-17, the flak hit the No. 2 engine, tearing it off. The aircraft then broke into several sections as it tumbled down. He could not imagine anyone escaping. Miraculously Major Jones and two gunners bailed out, becoming POWs, but the rest of the crew, including my last minute replacement, navigator Lt. Guertin, did not make it.[40] This proved to me that there were no easy missions or "milk runs".

Again I wondered how I could have been so miraculously saved. I thanked the Lord but yet I deeply mourned for those who had died in my place. Equally, I grieved for Gene Arning, with whom I had shared this most successful mission to Cottbus a few days earlier. These outstanding men had made the ultimate sacrifice that we knew could happen to us at any time.

In order to get our minds off the continuing horrors of combat, we would at least attempt to get off our base. When we knew that we had no mission a couple of buddies and I would take bicycle rides. I especially recall the beauty of the deep red roses by some of the houses. Also as we stopped to admire an old thatched-roof house, the owner invited us in, even taking us upstairs as he explained the construction of the roof. When children saw us coming out they gathered around exclaiming "any gum, chum?" I have pictures showing how our former Squadron Navigator, Capt. Stickel, whom I had succeeded, and I responded positively to their requests. It was a wonderful diversion to be among these friendly people and to absorb the beauty of nature for a few hours.

"Any gum, chum?"

24th mission – Berlin:
April 29, 1944

I thought when I started flying Wing leads it would always be as the lead crew in our 535th Squadron. However, as a Squadron Navigator, I learned on this mission to Berlin that I would sometimes be selected to fly with a Pathfinder (PFF) bomber crew when our Group led the Wing. Two crews from our 381st Bomb Group had been sent to train with this new PFF equipment at another base, but they returned to our base when needed for missions deep into Germany. One of these crews had Capt. Carl Clark, formerly of the 532nd Squadron, as the pilot. Col. David Kunkel, CO of the 534th, sitting in the co-pilot's seat, was chosen to lead this entire 1st Combat Wing formation. There was also a PFF navigator in the radio room in case the bombardier could not bomb visually.

When the Intelligence officer pulled aside the curtain at briefing, he pointed out that our target was the Erkner ball-bearing plant near Berlin. We had good fighter cover in and out, the flak was not too heavy and our bombing results were good. The fact that we had been able to go deep into the Reich without losing any bomber was good for our morale for the time being!

I recall an experience on the way to the target. When I was preparing my flight plan, I drew in our proposed route on strip maps. Then, as always, I checked my little "flak map" (see mission 16) and saw that we would be flying over one of my previously experienced flak areas. About 30 miles from that area I asked the pilot to take a heading of 30 degrees to the right. As the Colonel could see the ground from the co-pilot's seat and was following our course on his map, he hesitated and said, "But Navigator, you're taking us off course." I replied, "I know, Colonel, but if you wish to go through the flak ahead, it will be your responsibility when we get back on the ground." He said, "OK Navigator" and took my heading. When we were about 5 miles to the right and just out of the range of the flak cloud, I gave the headings to get us back on track. He and the crew as well as many other crews were quite amazed and expressed that they were grateful for an experienced navigator. Thanks again to my little "flak map"! Had we rigorously followed what we had been told and unnecessarily gone through that mass of exploding shells, we could have had much damage to both craft and crew of our 54-bomber formation. During interrogation back at the base, Col. Kunkel proudly mentioned our diversion from the planned route!

Lt. Col. David Kunkel

Homdrom returning from a combat mission
US Air Force photo, reprinted with permission

25th Mission – Leipzig:
May 12, 1944

Again I was to lead the Wing with the pilot, Capt. Carl Clark in a PFF ship, but this time our own 535th Squadron CO Col. Charles L. (Roy) Halsey, flew as Wing leader and our co-pilot. The industrial area near Leipzig was a long distance away, but fortunately no bomber or crew member was lost from our Group. We were pleased with the good bombing results that we trusted would further hamper the German war effort.

When we had arrived at our base in 1943, we were told that we could go back to America after 25 missions. Then we were notified that the total for a tour had recently been raised to 30. Fortunately, our war against the German Luftwaffe, both in the air and on the ground against their effort to produce more fighter planes, had borne fruit. Secondly, the addition of the long-range P51 fighters (Mustangs) had made for fewer bomber losses on long missions. Yet one couldn't help but wonder, "Can I survive five more missions?" Nevertheless, I was confident that with my experience I was valuable to the 381st Bomb Group's effort to assist in defeating Germany. Above all I knew that the Lord who had been with me through so much danger would see me through my tour - if it was his will.

At return from mission. Interrogation by Intelligence officers. Major DeLano, Group Navigator, standing in rear, Homdrom with navigator's log sitting,. Col. Halsey in center

US Air Force photo, reprinted with permission

103

26th Mission – Leipzig:
May 28, 1944

Again I was to lead the 1st Combat Wing to a target near Leipzig, but this time we had a familiar former crew from our 535th Squadron, that of Capt. Jim Tyson. When he and his crew arrived at our base after their flight across the Atlantic, they began flying in our Squadron. The four officers, including the navigator, John Howland, moved into our quanset hut. John was nearly three years younger than I and showed great promise as an excellent navigator. About mid-March that crew was sent to the PFF School to study navigation through the clouds. We were grateful that such new aids were constantly being developed, because many a mission had been a failure due to clouds over the target area.

From take-off, gathering in squadron, group and wing formation, arriving at rendezvous points with various groups of escort fighters and up to the beginning of the bomb run we had fulfilled the flight plan perfectly. But haze and smoke screen over the refinery prevented the bombardier from pinpointing the target. We then bombed an airport east of Leipzig. At any rate it was a fairly successful mission against the German industrial potential with no loss from our Group.

Between the last mission on the 12th and this one, I had had a much-needed leave of 7 days in a wonderful old country estate called Roke Manor, which was run by the Red Cross. From my brother Clarence's APO address, I surmised that he had been on his way to England. Prior to my leave departure, I found out that I might inquire at the Supreme Allied Headquarters in London to ask if Clarence's Engineering Camouflage Battalion had arrived. As I approached Grosvenor Square, I was stopped by a military police guard. Satisfied with my credentials, he led me to an upstairs room, informing the officer of my request. "Yes, they just arrived", he said and pointed on the huge map to a forest about 100 miles west where they were bivouacked. What a wonderful reunion we had after my trip by train and finally by an MP Jeep. Imagine his surprise! To obtain such secret information was, I believe, a privilege only available to officers. It was very special.

As they were having a gas mask drill, they lent me a bicycle. Apparently after the danger I had gone through, I found this boring, so after awhile I tried riding sitting on the seat backwards. Did I ever take a tumble! My hands were badly bruised and even the knee of my OD pink (olive drab officer's dress) trousers was torn. With bandaged hands I arrived at the rest home thinking that all would believe I had had a rough combat mission; however, when the snippy Red Cross girl saw me and asked, "What's the matter, Lieutenant, were you hurt on a bicycle?" I was too embarrassed to answer. I guess we needed this kind of treatment to bring us to a state of relaxation. I really was sorry that the bandaged hands prevented me from joining in on the softball games because I enjoy that sport. At any rate I could be the umpire. Those 7 days with wonderful food, good fellowship and rest were really helpful to reduce the stress that I believe all of us had experienced. Truly there was nothing quite so beautiful as to see the Red Cross girls, always ready with a smile and some conversation. It had been a much-needed break, but it was back to four more combat missions before I could really relax. Each one could mean injury, becoming a POW or even death. However, I could not spend time thinking about such possibilities. I had to concentrate on my work as Squadron Navigator - whether it was on the ground training replacement navigators or any assignments in the air.

With brother Clarence Homdrom in England
before D-Day

Roke Manor - Red Cross run rest home

27th Mission – Paris, France: June 2, 1944

Finally I was to fly with Capt. Charles Enos, who was listed with me and seven others as the lead crew of the 535th Squadron. Our Squadron CO Col. Halsey was to lead the Wing sitting in the co-pilot's position. I was especially happy to fly with and be part of this best group of crewmen in our 535th Bomb Squadron. For the 3rd day the targets were in France, so naturally there were many rumors as to the impending invasion of Europe. Even passes were cancelled indefinitely. With good visibility on this mission, we had excellent bombing results in spite of moderate flak. Some Groups bombed Boulogne while others bombed Paliseau, both airfields near Paris. [41]

As I approached the tour limit of 30 missions, I was happy to fly with one of our most reliable pilots. But I could sense that he was more tense as he also approached the end of his tour. On the ground he was virtually a chain smoker, finishing two packets of cigarettes a day, but in the air he wasn't fazed by anything. With fighters coming at us, he would call on the intercom, "Hey, fellows, do you see those pretty yellow things out there?" Of course those pretty yellow things were the explosive shells the German pilots were firing at us. But when we got to the ground, he would say to me, "Ted, I can't understand how you can remain so calm without even smoking." I can give a lot of credit for that to my faith and the knowledge that so many were praying for me. Also, though, it helped a lot for me to be concentrating on instruments and the navigator's log. I didn't have to look out most of the time like the gunners, bombardier and even the pilots.

As a rule, we as the lead crew only flew combat when our squadron led the entire wing of 54 Flying Fortresses. However, on other days when there was a mission, Enos and I would rotate with the three other squadron lead crews to fly the weather ship. We would fly to different altitudes and points over England, reporting back to base the heights and other characteristics of the clouds. This would assist in deciding what altitudes the squadron, group and wing formations would assemble prior to departure over the North Sea or English Channel for the continent. Because we had such opportunities, we had an agreement that I should teach him navigation and he would teach me something about how to fly the bomber. The closest I came to an actual landing was when I let down on a cloud! It was a real privilege to have such opportunities with this good friend. One other recollection was when Col. Halsey asked us to fly him to a friend. She somehow had obtained something that was not on the list of rations – steaks! Even if it was most likely through the Black Market, it certainly was a tremendous treat for us. Thus there were occasional privileges along with our responsibilities.

28th Mission – Normandy Beach, Caen, France: D-DAY June 6, 1944

About 10pm on June 5th, we lead pilots, navigators and bombardiers were called to Group Headquarters. As we had never before been called out in the evening, we sensed that something big was about to happen. As our Group CO Col. Harry Leber pulled aside the curtain on the map in the briefing room, he pointed to the Normandy coast and said, "Well, men, this is it!"

He said the plan for us would be to go in with squadrons of six planes. We would only have a 6-mile wide corridor in which to form and fly over the channel. Also he emphasized the absolute necessity of clockwork, because, immediately after the bombs were dropped, the men would be storming the beaches from their variety of boats. We navigators then worked the next few hours until an early breakfast to make, check and recheck our flight plans. We did not want to drop bombs on our men. They already would be facing all sorts of bombardment, mines and obstacles in attempting to land and establish a beachhead into Nazi-held territory.

Another unusual part of our briefing was that for the first time we were issued with pistols. In case we were forced down, we could then at least temporarily attempt to join the men fighting on the ground - or escape. There was also the most severe warning that we were not to breathe this information about the invasion to anyone, not even other crew members or ground personnel.

We had been told at this evening briefing that much activity would happen before our bombs would be dropped - such as the glider borne troops and paratroopers landing further inland shortly after midnight. But when we advanced across, on that historic D-Day mission, nine-tenths cloud covered the English Channel. I wondered if this exhaustive Invasion was actually proceeding – until through a hole in the clouds I saw a massive array of boats of all sizes and shapes heading for the continent. I was pleased that we were the squadron lead crew, including Capt. Enos as pilot. At 14,000 ft. this was our lowest height for a bombing strike over Europe. Although it was one of the shortest missions for us to return from after hearing the bombardier say "Bombs away!", we were deeply concerned for the men storming the beaches. Knowing that so many would lose their lives below us, we prayed that they would be able to establish a beachhead.

Originally the Supreme Commander Dwight Eisenhower had decided that the Invasion should take place on June 5th, but due to the bad weather he postponed it. To have attempted the Invasion that day would have been a complete disaster. Never before in history had such a massive military force been assembled for an attack – upon a fortified area, so it was a gamble on Eisenhower's part. Even on the next day weather conditions were far from favorable, but if it had not taken place then, it was said that "Operation Warlord" would have had to wait perhaps three or four more weeks. Such a delay could jeopardize the chances for the Allied forces' advance into Germany before winter. Consequently, this was it – D-Day! We in the 381st Bomb Group were appropriately a part of this increasingly anticipated historic mission. How we waited for reports as to how this gigantic venture would fare for the next couple of days! Thank God, the beachhead had been established. But at what a cost! Spielberg's movie, "Saving Private Ryan", depicts quite realistically what the men on the ground went through.[42] We in our Group who had bombed the coast were pleased to hear that in spite of the clouds below, not one of our bombs had fallen in the water. Not everything in that massive undertaking went according to plan, but at least our bombing had assisted in this historic venture. I was proud to be a part of it.

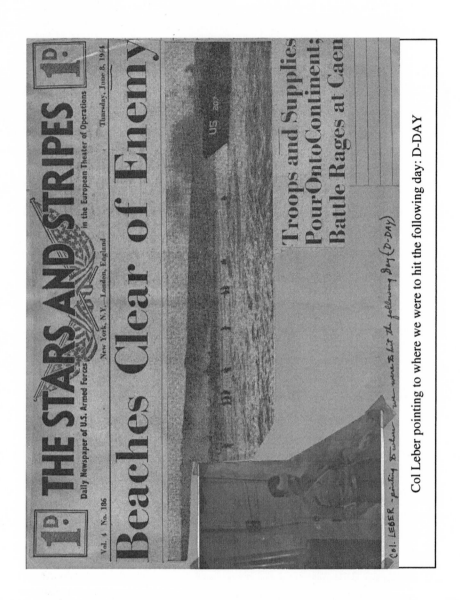

Col Leber pointing to where we were to hit the following day: D-DAY

29th Mission – Paris, France:
June 14, 1944

Again we as the lead crew of the 535th Squadron, including pilot Enos and Col. Halsey, led the Wing. This was a tactical effort to hinder the German efforts in their attempts to prevent the Allies from advancing inland. In spite of the success of the Invasion, Germany continued to bring strong forces to endeavor to contain the Allies. Consequently we were given certain targets such as airfields which had been taken by the Germans earlier. Our targets, Melun and Villaroche airfields near Paris, were badly damaged. We were pleased that all of our aircraft returned safely. However, from the limited media we knew that the ground forces were still having a rough time breaking through the German defenses. Nevertheless, the ingenious floating ports had greatly assisted the movement of supplies necessary for a massive advance toward Germany.

As I reminisce about my last two missions, I more recently had the opportunity to visit the area of the Invasion. A doctor friend, with his wife and son, from Holland were visiting us in February 1995 when one night mention was made of D-Day on the TV. I merely remarked that I should have been at Normandy the previous June 6th to celebrate the 50th anniversary of D-Day with many others that had taken part in the Invasion. Dr. Hammer then said, "Well, just come and visit us and we'll take you there." They also showed eagerness to visit that historic site. A few months later this trip materialized. Being actually on the ground to see our bomb craters, the German emplacements and their underground tunnels and so much more was very impressive. The museums recreated much to help us to understand the many phases in planning and carrying out the tremendous undertaking. But what was most emotional for me to see was the rows upon rows of crosses of the thousands who had died to establish the necessary foothold. May God bless their memory!

30th Mission – Berlin:
June 21, 1944

Having completed 29 combat missions over Europe – a few in which I had been almost miraculously spared – I could not help but ponder, can I get through one more to complete my tour? On the morning of June 21st, I was told that I was to fly Wing lead one more time with Col. Halsey as Wing leader and Capt. Tyson as pilot in a Pathfinder plane. I was also to have the assistance of the pathfinder navigator, Lt. John Howland, to help with navigational calculations. As the log had to remain with the 535th Squadron, I cannot give as many details as I would like.

We were told at the briefing that, after several tactical raids to assure the success of the Invasion, we would now return to our pounding of the strategic targets deep in Germany. Our target for this, my last mission, was again the "Big-B". This time it was the Luftwaffe headquarters and the other government buildings. While preparing the flight plan during the usual three hours prior to take-off, I didn't have time to think about possible danger - even though we were reminded of the heavy flak near the Luftwaffe headquarters. We, of course, were aware as always that the flak gunners below would certainly zero in on the lead plane in order to attempt to disrupt the mission.

From take-off, gathering in formation, arriving at the enemy coast and rendezvousing with most of the various groups of escort fighters up to the Initial Point (IP) before the bomb run, our mission had gone exactly as planned to the minute at every spot. For a short while when a group of our escort fighters failed to arrive, we were viscously attacked by a group of over 50 enemy aircraft. 20 mm. shells were exploding all around us; several B-17s were shot down. During our entire journey in our visibility was partially hampered by contrail formations from a previous group as well as haze conditions below.

After I had reported our arrival at the IP to the Colonel, I gave the pilot the heading for the bomb run to the target about 40 miles away. He immediately called out: "OK, Bombardier, take over." The autopilot was then transferred to his Norden bombsight. Putting on my steel helmet and checking my flak vest, I made my log complete to that moment and noted in my mind the next heading from the target. I decided after a couple of minutes to stand to the rear and right and look over the shoulder of our pathfinder bombardier, Lt. Eager, to see if he was indeed zeroing in on Hitler's establishment. As we approached the heavy flak cloud, a small chunk about the size of an egg came from the bottom and out through the top of the plexiglass nose, missing Eager's head by inches. However, without even moving his head, he kept right on concentrating on lining up the hairs of the bombsight with the target. The success of our objective now depended on him. When I saw how accurate the flak was, I covered my left eye with my hand. Seconds later a huge chunk of flak hit the bottom of the window about a foot from my head. It pulverized the window, going out the ceiling in half a dozen jagged holes. The glass bits hit the back of my unprotected hand and neck and one piece bounced off my oxygen mask under my glasses, injuring my right eye. When we heard "Bombs away!", I gave the pilot the heading to begin our return journey. By now my vision was blurred by some moisture. I wasn't certain whether it was blood, sweat or tears, but I had responded with the heading for the return journey.

After flying on the heading that I had given for a few minutes, Eager turned around for something. Seeing my bleeding injuries, he immediately called on the intercom "The navigator's been injured!" The Colonel then told Eager to attend to my wounds while Howland followed the flight plan back to England. It was good to have a sharp navigator like him to do this. It was also the final mission of his tour.

Shortly after the bombs were dropped, the pilot attempted to return the ship that had been controlled from the bombsight by autopilot to the plane's regular controls. However, gunners reported severed control cables hanging near them; consequently the pilot was forced to return to auto pilot. It was fortunate that we in our damaged plane were leading, because we could not have attempted to fly formation off the other planes' lead on autopilot. Instead the huge formation continued following our steady and level lead back to England.

We were not the only casualty. On the bomb run to the target, 2nd Lt. Roger Dussault and crew were shot down and were later reported POWs. The heavy flak punched holes in 27 of the remaining 37 B-17s of our Group. After Lt. Roy Pendergist's plane had dropped its bombs, it began burning from a direct hit. Just before it exploded, Roy and his crew had bailed out, but three enlisted men were killed. A plane flown by Lt. Art Bailey lost 2 engines from the fighter attacks but managed to land in Sweden.[43] Meanwhile, a crew from our squadron faced a different crisis. A fire in the cockpit caused Lt. Myerscough to be smothered in burning hydraulic fluid. Fortunately Sgt. Rolla's quick reaction saved the pilot's life by smothering the flames with his hands and putting out the fire. In spite of their burns, the pilots nursed the Fortress back to our base. Having lost the fluid, the pilots successfully halted the plane with parachutes from the rear as it touched down on the runway. The few examples above give an idea of the many possible crises bomber crews faced.

Even though one could assume that once over England a flyer had safely completed his mission, he could be mistaken. Not too surprisingly, Col. Halsey called us on the intercom, "Men, we have a problem. We can't guarantee that we can land safely on auto pilot, so we'll give you a choice - to bail out or take a chance with the ship." We all opted for the latter. After a practice landing on a cloud, the pilot went in for a perfect landing! What a way to finish my tour!

Though I was injured, I was asked if I could manage to accompany Col. Halsey through interrogation before I went to the hospital. I agreed because only I could give details from my log on all incidents of the mission. Thereafter the Jeep driver took me to the base hospital. The Flight Surgeon told me that I had been very fortunate – only the white of my eye had been cut.

After a couple of days lying there, the nurse told me that a delegation with our Group Commander Col.

Leber had arrived. He, along with Brig. Gen. Gross from Division Headquarters, Maj. Gaylord, our Group Flight Surgeon and Lt. Col. Reed from Wing Headquarters, approached and stood around my bed while Col. Reed read a citation for the Oak Leaf Cluster to the Distinguished Flying Cross for the mission to Berlin.[44] He then, for my completed tour of 30 missions, pinned the DFC on my pajamas! It was one of the most thrilling moments of my life. I had not only survived my tour but I had received such a high recognition of achievement for that mission. I also would receive the usual medal for being wounded in action – the Purple Heart.

After a week in the hospital I could return to my barracks and tidy up my Squadron Navigator's office. In doing statistics, I found that since my arrival in my squadron, we had had 27 navigators no longer on the roster to fly combat. Only four of us completed our tour. Of those four, three of us had received the Purple Heart! It was good to join my friends in the Officers' Club and officers' mess. While I still had the bandage over my eye, I was told that the actor Edward G. Robinson was visiting our base. When he saw me in the mess hall, he joined our table and wanted to know all about how my injury had occurred. He had a deep concern for all of us as he spoke to our whole Group as well. Visits by celebrities such as he, Bob Hope and many others, both male and female, were very uplifting.

Before leaving our base to return to America, my promotion to Captain came through. Major Delano, our Group Navigator, on leaving for the US while I was in the hospital, wrote, "Congratulations on the double DFC".[45] 55 years later at the first reunion of the 381st Bomb Group I thanked him for his letter! I couldn't answer before, because I didn't have his address.

Initially I was sent to Wales to await the return trip to the US. While there those days with no official duties, I met a lovely girl called "Flick", with whom I did some sightseeing. It was interesting to learn a bit of Welsh, which she spoke fluently. Had I been stationed there for some time I later wondered how our relationship would have developed. Would I have ended up with a wife from the British Isles? I also observed a poker game that showed how carefree the men were. With the smallest denomination being a $20 bill or the equivalent, a five-pound note, the pile in the center of the table had several hundred dollars. The golfing celebrity Bobby Jones was also enthusiastically involved in the game.

Because of my rank as Captain, I was told that on the ship back to America I would be in charge of several hundred men. However, because this responsibility didn't appeal to me and because I was also eager to return home, I jumped at the opportunity to join 59 other returning servicemen on an aircraft, even if we heard that the same kind of plane (a C-54, I believe) which had left the day before, had completely disappeared! What a surprise when we boarded to find that we were to sit in uncomfortable bucket seats all around the outside wall of the plane. And of course there was no stewardess!

Stopping in Iceland for fuel, we also had a memorable meal with "white" bread - something we had never seen due to strict rationing in England. We all would have liked to at least spend another day there, but naturally we had to go when the plane had refueled.

Over 50 years later while I have been attempting to write up these "Mission Memories" of my military service – training and combat – I have often awakened quite early and been unable to go back to sleep. Just reliving those experiences most probably is one of the reasons why I have been reluctant to talk about them much all these years. Jeffrey L. Ethall wrote this regarding war casualties: "Statistically there was no more dangerous place to be in World War II than in a bomber over Germany."[46] Our children now say that they did not know much about what I went through.

In retrospect I've often marveled how so many experiences, such as growing up poor, subjects learned in school, work experiences and the like have remarkably prepared me for what I would face later in life. Majoring in history and having many math courses certainly were very helpful for navigation. I personally feel that the Lord always prepared me for what I would later encounter in his leading.

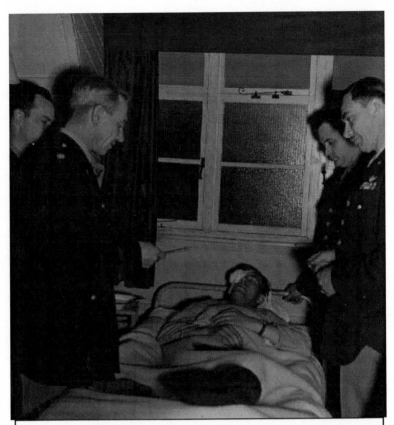

Left to right: Col. Leber, Col. Reed (reading citation Appendix A),
Homdrom, Major Gaylord, Gen. Gross
US Air Force photo, reprinted with permission

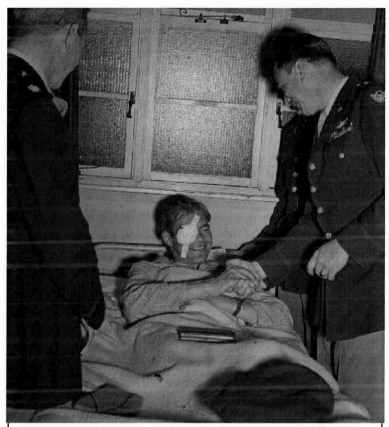

Gen. Gross congratulating Homdrom after pinning the DFC on his
pajamas in Army Air Force hospital
US Air Force photo, reprinted with permission

Back in America

Home Leave and Redistribution Center

Arriving the next morning in Bangor, Maine, we were told that we were now on our own. What a thrill to be back in America after what I had gone through the past 8 or 9 months! I hitched a ride on a military plane to New York, where I took in the glittering lights. Having a steak dinner at Jack Dempsey's Café was really a treat. All the people were so friendly. I also ordered an Eisenhower-type battle jacket at Saks Fifth Avenue store. From there it was by train and bus with a stop in Chicago to my home in Erskine, Minnesota. On the bus from Minneapolis I met De Etta, an attractive nurse. We saw each other whenever possible for the next year or so.

As I wasn't certain when I would arrive home, I hadn't phoned my mother, but I found her outside. Having received the telegram that her son had been wounded, she couldn't believe her eyes when she saw me walking toward her. It was a thrilling reunion with her and so many others who had prayed and been concerned about my safety. However, it was almost impossible to settle down to such a quiet life for those 15 days. When I was in the barber's shop, I barely kept from exploding when I heard a farmer bragging about how he had kept his son from being drafted. Yet he was criticizing the military for the way they were conducting the war. I was at the point of volunteering for another tour of combat! Some of the people in the Midwest were so indifferent to the war. I felt that the English people were in the war effort as much as we service personnel were. I recall a sign in one London store window reading, "We're open until 6pm unless we're hit." Bombing by the V-1 buzz bombs and later by the V-2 bombs could happen anytime and anywhere.

When my leave was over, I was fortunate to have a booking to Miami on a very fine air-conditioned train called the South Wind. The two-week stay in what would have been considered a luxury hotel was meant for more rest for us returnees and finally reassignment at the Redistribution Center. It wasn't surprising that some combat veterans had a difficult time readjusting to such a quiet life. The 4th navigator – the only one not wounded in action – in our squadron who had completed his tour was of Polish descent; he had a bitter hatred for the Germans. I don't know how he got a pistol in England, probably at a London pawnshop. I found out later that he was the only one who flew combat with it before D-Day.[47] He told us that if he ever had to bail out, he would kill as many "Krauts" as he could. We knew he had this passion when he volunteered and flew an extra mission after his 30th. To any of the rest of us who had sweated out the last mission, this was proof that he was a bit "tetched in the haid". When we had completed our tours, we had to turn in all equipment. Before D-Day, those returning were actually searched. The ball turret gunner in our original crew told me he that he managed to save some valuable personal photos in combat because he had them in a secret hiding place in his luggage. In Miami we soon learned that Hallowenski had been able to smuggle his pistol through.

One night he took the gun from his luggage and shot out the chandelier in our beautiful seaside hotel room! For that he had to go for observation in Section 8 until they would be certain that he was back to normal. John Coomer wrote about the treatment as follows: "In severe cases of neurosis, and continuing anxiety, injections of sodium pentathol were used, along with the help of a psychologist, to pry troublesome memories out of the subconscious mind. The patient was induced to talk at great length about those nightmarish experiences. The drug helped to release the deeply buried tensions. Most times it worked."[48] In a sense, then, the combat toll for us navigators in the 381st Bomb Group while I was there had been 100%. Fortunately, however, most of those who had completed their tour or had been POWs eventually were able to resume normal lives.

Back to Monroe Navigation School

Now that I had completed a tour overseas, I wondered where the Army Air Corps would reassign me. The first step was to send me back to Monroe, Louisiana, where I would receive some orientation for possible assignment in the United States.

From Miami I had a nice ride to New Orleans with a colleague of the 381st Bomb Group, Lt. "Whitey" Evans. He had purchased a snazzy convertible on his stay at Miami and was keen to have some company. It was a really scenic trip along the Gulf with a stop at New Orleans. What a contrast to what we had gone through during those previous months.

When I arrived at Monroe, I was received by my former instructors with mixed feelings, I believe. Now that I was a captain while they were still lieutenants, they would be sent overseas to go into combat - if we returnees replaced them. However, this did not happen immediately because they had to give us our orientation for teaching.

This was an enjoyable period. Having had overseas flying pay, I had enough money to buy one of the latest models produced, a 1941 Model Ford. Because of automakers' conversion to manufacturing tanks, they only began making automobiles again in 1946.

Another enjoyable part of being in Monroe, without very strict responsibilities, was the social life. There was a Lutheran church that I attended in the town. The organist was Elna, a young widow who had lost her navigator husband in combat. Without a pastor, we servicemen took turns preaching. After services there was always some sort of social function, such as swimming or a picnic. It was good to have a break from strictly military associations.

One problem with having a car was gas rationing – only 15 gallons per month. When I was reassigned to another navigation school in San Marcos, Texas, with a 15-day delay en route via my home in Minnesota, I worried about having enough gasoline for the trip. At a party I met a young lady who gave me coupons for 15 more gallons. Then also I had riders from Minnesota who helped with their ration. Along the way a couple of filling stations waived the requirement when I explained how short I was running. It helped when they saw the ribbons on my uniform. They were happy to assist a veteran who had been in combat. Consequently we had sufficient fuel to make the 1,300-mile trip. On the way I also had a nice visit with De Etta. It was good to be home for Christmas. While home, Uncle Arne Landsverk, a farmer, gave me coupons for 60 gallons, which he didn't need for his tractor in the winter. Thus our fuel problem was solved for our trip south to Texas. Another shortage was tires. I was really shocked when we arrived at our new base to see that two of the tires were down to the thread. How lucky not to have had a blowout! However, these could be, actually had to be, retreaded, because new tires were virtually unobtainable. The war was still going on in the Pacific.

San Marcos Navigation School

Being assigned as an instructor brought back happy memories. After all, I had been a high school teacher when I was drafted about three years earlier. When I arrived at the San Marcus Navigation School in Texas at the end of December 1944, I was appointed as assistant commander in a flight of 10 instructors and 60 aviation cadets. They had five weeks remaining in their advanced training course. I was glad that I was not immediately assigned as commander. One captain who arrived at the same time as I did received the full responsibility of a flight. Because over 100 instructors were sent overseas for combat duty the week before, it was quite a mix-up at this school. Immediately I was assigned to fly with students on practical navigation missions. The flights with three students were in twin-engine twin-tail Beachcraft training airplanes, usually about 300 miles from San Marcos.

One exception came when I had been there only about two weeks. The flight to which I had been assigned had won the War Bond contest, giving it the privilege of using a training flight to Hollywood. This was quite an undertaking – 18 planes with a pilot, three cadets and an instructor in each. I had to take the three poorest students. It was their final test. Realizing that other lives would depend on their navigating ability, I washed out the two who in my judgment were absolutely hopeless.

Because the entire country was behind the war effort, a splendid program had been planned for us. We had a reserved section at the Earl Carroll Theater for one event. Likewise we had the front seats on a live national broadcast – there was no TV yet – with Danny Kaye and the Harry James Orchestra! What a treat for these cadets – and also, of course, for us instructors.

Because of a day's delay due to fog, I had the opportunity to visit my cousin Goodie Landsverk once again. My last visit had been about two years earlier when I was stationed in California with the 5th Armored Division. She was really amazed to see all the combat ribbons on my uniform. She like so many other women was employed in some war industry.

The living conditions for officers at this school did not come up to the high standards at all the previous places where I had been serving. We had to clean our rooms and even buy our own furniture, such as bureaus for our clothing. Our ration for gas was only 10 gallons per month. This didn't help much in this state of long distances. At least it was much better for me than being back in combat.

The period as assistant flight commander was short-lived. After three weeks my commander went on leave – leaving me in charge. On January 28, 1945, I wrote home, "What a busy week! I can't remember when I've worked so hard. The hardest part is that I don't know enough about the job of running a flight; it stands to reason that it must be considered fairly hard when some instructors don't get to be flight commanders after working over two years as an instructor. Besides being a very busy week, we had to get everything spick and span for an Inspector General. I had to attend many flight commander meetings as well…. He won't be back for two weeks, and by then this flight will graduate." Perhaps one or two of my experienced instructors who were still lieutenants could have fulfilled that position better than I could, but the Army Air Corps had to give me an assignment equivalent to my rank! Nevertheless, my position as Squadron Navigator overseas had given me much administrative experience even for this type of a position.[49]

The final week before graduation was less strenuous with much excitement on the part of the cadets who were about to be graduating as "an officer and a gentleman". They appreciated that I attended their party for a while, especially because the ribbons on my jacket demonstrated a great deal of experience in combat.

On that weekend when the class members had left, a friend and I went to Austin where we enjoyed a movie, church and bowling – I had one score of 236 with an average of nearly 200! It was tremendously refreshing for both body and soul to have such a good break.

After the graduation, another 60 cadets arrived for their training. I would not teach the pre-flight courses, but I set up a schedule for my instructors. Consequently, I was free to go on some instructor-directed flights. The one to Chicago in mid-February was supposed to last 60 hours, but it was hampered by fog and low clouds. After an overnight delay in Kansas City, we proceeded to Chicago the next day. As we were delayed again, I observed in the entertainment section of the paper that the much listened to national radio network program, "The Hour of Charm", with the Phil Spitalni orchestra, was to perform there that night. A Concordia College classmate of mine, Meda Westburg, called Francini, was the lead soloist, with her low alto voice.

Arriving a bit early for the performance, I took up courage to go back stage and hesitatingly asked if it would be possible to see Meda. This is what I wrote home, "She was so glad to see me that she got me up in the first row for the performance. When she had sung her solo, she came down and sat through the rest of the show with me. Everyone envied me and yet she thought she was the lucky one, imagine that? She really went for me, wanting to write and get me to come to New York sometime on a flight." A week or so later she phoned me saying she was worried that something had happened to me. She had heard that an airplane similar to the one in which we had flown had crashed killing all on board. I did visit her later in New York, but I soon realized that our life styles were very different. At any rate I was not ready to be serious about marriage until the war was over.

Officers Command and Training School

During those weeks of training more navigators, I was also closely following the progress of the war. After the winter setback of the Battle of the Bulge, the Allied tanks and infantry were finally advancing again toward the heart of the Reich. When about 15 of us combat veterans were sent to the Officers' Command and Training School in San Antonio for a month's course in mid-March, I was wondering what they had in mind for us. The officer in charge, Col. J.M. Hutchinson, addressed us, telling us how valuable we with our combat experience would be in the molding of future officers and navigators. When a picture of the entire group with all of our combat ribbons was taken, he said, "This is the closest I've been to combat!" He only had his wings – which we all also had, but his were pilot wings.

The course stressed exactly how things should be done and how important neatness was. One example was how our wings should be placed on our battle-jacket or blouse. They should be ½ inch below the coat lapel, parallel to the ground. Similar instructions were given for our combat ribbons. They checked such things at inspections. Col. Hutchinson went on to point out the value of combat returnees in the important phases of the training program by explaining that they were able to suggest changes which should make the course more practical. He also hinted that we might be assigned different jobs when we were through. Having only classes to attend, rather than to prepare for, gave us time to visit historical sights – like the famous Alamo.

We were also aware of the great advances of the Allies toward Berlin. There was the significant news that in February 1945, Roosevelt, Stalin and Churchill met at Yalta to discuss problems. Some of the agreements reached had long-lasting repercussions – leading to the Cold War. We also had heard that Germany was in flames. Thus, some of us returnees were a bit light-hearted as we marched and sang with lines such as "Left, left, I had a good job but I left; left, left, I had a good wife but she left!" When we finished the course in San Antonio, we heard the shocking news that President Roosevelt had died – on April 12, 1945. We couldn't imagine Truman in any way taking over, but we soon learned that he was quite able. Nearly a month later was V-E Day – on May 7, 1945.

Officers' Command and Training School. Homdrom is third from left front row. Col. Hutchinson is center front
US Air Force photo, reprinted with permission

Honorable Discharge

We wondered if that could mean the end of the war for us, but no, we had a long way yet to go against Japan. However, the Army Air Force realized that there were enough flying personnel trained to carry on in the Pacific and decided to allow some to be discharged.

A point system was offered allowing persons with 72 points to request their discharge from the service. There was a point for each month in the service, several points for being married, several points for each medal award, etc. Because of all the medals I had been awarded, my total was 92 points. Consequently, I could apply for my discharge, but it was not an easy decision. With captain's salary plus 50% additional flying pay, I could not hope to earn that much in civilian life. I finally told myself, "Being drafted, you did not request to join the armed forces. Therefore why don't you just take this first chance to get out?" I figured that mathematically I could not hope to live through another tour of combat. If it hadn't been for the Lord and his guardian angel I wouldn't have lasted through the one I completed. It also looked like the war against Japan could not last very much longer, and, if so, I didn't want to make a career of the military service. I really didn't know what I wanted to do. I still resisted the idea of going into the ministry, even though the Holy Spirit would from time to time remind me of my promise on my 14th mission. Thus, at the age of 26, after three and a quarter years in the service, I asked for my discharge. I decided, at least for the near future, to do some graduate work in history at the University of Minnesota and possibly to begin thinking of marriage. Here, too, I would continue to look for someone who would be willing to follow the Lord's leading.

All in all, my time spent in the Service had been great. I was pleased that I had heeded the call of my country and that I was able to take part in defeating the enemy that had been selfish for land and ruthless against people. For us it was a popular war supported by the American people.

For me personally I had so much to be grateful for. I had learned so much about the world from all the travel. I had learned to know so many wonderful people, both men and women. Also, the Service had developed my leadership qualities, which were to help me later in life. I couldn't help but believe that the Lord had seen me through for some reason. What would follow these "Mission Memories"?

Appendix A: Memorabilia

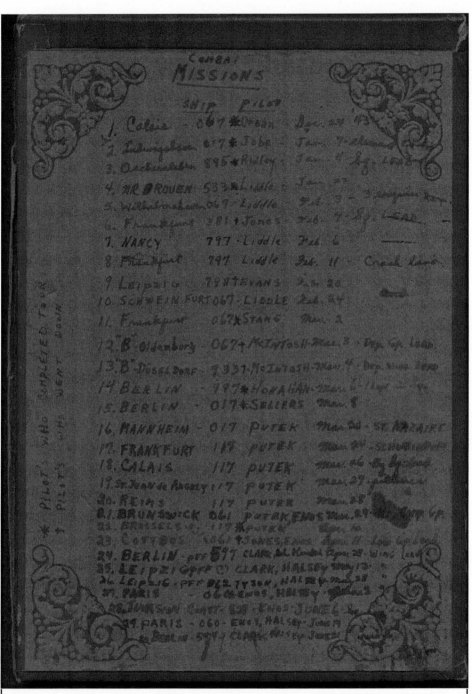

Copy of Personal Writing Pad Blotter with 30 Combat Missions

II. Under the provisions of Army Regulations 600-45, 22 September 1943, as amended and pursuant to authority contained in letter, Hq Eighth Air Force, File 200.6, 1 June 1944, subject, "Awards and Decorations," and OAK LEAF CLUSTER is awarded to the following-named Officer for wear with the DISTINGUISHED FLYING CROSS previously awarded.

*   *   *

THEODORE (NMI) HOMDROM, O-809611, First Lieutenant, Air Corps, United States Army. For extraordinary achievement while serving as Navigator in the lead airplane of a Combat Bombardment Wing of B-17 aircraft on a bombing mission over Germany, 21 June 1944. From the beginning of the climb to altitude through the assembly and most of the journey to and from the target visibility was seriously hampered by contrail formations and haze conditions at altitude and on the ground. Before the bombing run the formation was subjected to vicious attacks by a large force of enemy aircraft and, as the turn on the bombing run was made, anti-aircraft fire was brought to bear on the formation, painfully wounding Lieutenant Homdrom and damaging the Aircraft in which he flew. Despite pain and discomfort, Lieutenant Homdrom remained at his post to check for identification points along the bomb run and through the clearing smoke was able to identify the target. At this point a very short bombing run was made and bombs were dropped with great accuracy. In spite of his pain Lieutenant Homdrom remained at his task to assist in guiding the formation back to base. The courage, coolness and skill displayed by Lieutenant Homdrom reflect the highest credit upon himself and the Armed Forces of the United States. Entered military service from Minnesota.

By command of Major General WILLIAMS:

BARTLETT BEAMAN,
Brigadier General, U. S. Army,
Chief of Staff.

OFFICIAL:

/s/ Roberts P. Johnson, Jr.
ROBERTS P. JOHNSON, JR.,
Lieut. Colonel, A.G.D.,
Adjutant General.

A TRUE EXTRACT COPY:

THEODORE HOMDROM
Captain, A. C.

mfb

Copy of the Citation for the Oak Leaf Cluster to the Distinguished
Flying Cross

Presidential Distinguished Unit Citation

A Presidential Citation was awarded to the 1st Combat Group for "extraordinary heroism, determination and esprit de corps" on the January 11, 1944 mission to Oschersleben, Germany.

HEADQUARTERS
1ST COMBAT BOMBARDMENT GROUP
APO 557
200.6
11 August 1944

SUBJECT: Presidential Citation, 1st Bombardment Division
TO: Commanding Officers, 1st, 381st, & 398th Bombardment Groups

    1. The battle honors awarded the 1st Bombardment Division, by Section XI, WD General Orders No. 50, 17 June 1944, for extraordinary heroism, determination and esprit de corps, in bombing the heavily defended German Aircraft factories at Oschersleben, Germany, on the 11 January 1944, is a very high honor; it ranks with the DSC for individual heroism. In order fully to appreciate the meaning of this citation and the significance of the Distinguished Unit Badge now authorized for wear with the uniform in accordance with instructions contained in para. 4, Section IV, W.D. Circular 333, 22 December 1943, the full wing background and guidance of all personnel in the command.

    2. Oschersleben marked the beginning of our winning battle to cancel the fighter strength of the Luftwaffe by striking at the source of enemy air power: his airplane factories. It was fully understood by all, both by ourselves and by the enemy, that the winning of air mastery was a necessary prelude to victory. Without complete ownership of the air over the channel and the invasion coast, there could be no D-Day. It has become an

essential principle of warfare that surface contests between the major forces are decided by Air supremacy over the battlefield.

During the early history of the 8th Air Force, the American demonstrated that it was possible to conduct air operations over the continent in daylight and to make effective attacks on precision industrial targets. The threat to German war industry was clear, and the Hun promptly laid plans to meet it by projecting a fighter production to reach the staggering total of 2,500 fighter planes per month. Had that goal, easily within Germany's industrial power, ever been reached, the course of the war would have been far different from the events we are witnessing today.

During the preceding April, the 8th Air Force had knocked out the Focke-Wulf factory at Bremen. This led the Hun to withdraw his airplane factories from western Germany to places in the east where he thought they would be safe from air attack. He felt doubly safe when we suffered our heavy losses on Schweinfurt and Anklam in the fall of 1943. These places appeared at the outside of the range of our escort fighters, and effective air opposition forced us to temporarily desist from long-range attacks.

3. January 1944, Jerry's fighter program was getting into stride, while our long-range fighters were only beginning to come in, a small though encouraging trickle. Our problem was that if we waited for full-scale fighter support before daring to interrupt the German program, it might come too late. It may have been one of those cases where everything depended on a delicate question of timing and the ability to deliver a damaging blow before the opportunity was past.

Our target of the 11th January was the A.G.O. Aircraft factory Oschersleben This target is in the Magdeburg area, only 90 miles from Berlin. It was by all odds the deepest penetration ever made by our aircraft into the heart of Germany. The factory we were after was the most important unit in the network of timing and on the ability to deliver a damaging blow before the opportunity was past.

Our forces were smaller than they are now. Although it was a maximum effort for all groups, the Wing was able to scrape up only 63 airplanes. Three Combat Wings assigned to Oschersleben, the 1st, 41st and 94th, put up a total of 177 aircraft, and of these only 139 went through to attack the primary.

Weather over England and en route was much worse than anticipated. This made things rather bad. It broke up the Division order of battle, with the result that the 1st Combat Wing was obliged to proceed to the target alone, arriving in advance of the schedule leaders. The one group of P-51s then in the theater gave us target support as briefed, but the penetration and withdrawal support never materialized. The 2nd and 3rd Division, which were intended to dilute the fighter opposition en route by attacks in the Brunswick area, had to be recalled and only a few of their formation went through to their briefed targets.

As a result of these factors, the opposition we encountered from enemy fighters was probably the heaviest in the whole history of air warfare. The 1st Combat Wing, flying itself, bore the full share of the battle. The fight began in the vicinity of Dummer Lake, continued all the way to the target, including the bombing run and lasted after that until it had run over an hour and a half. Our Wing alone lost 13 of the total 42 aircraft lost by the Division. We were officially credited with 66 enemy aircraft destroyed, one probable and 145 damaged. Lt. Col. Milten, who was severely and painfully wounded an hour before the target, led our Wing formation to our target and back to England, where the entire Division was forced by weather to land at diversion airdromes. The lead airplanes had been severely damaged by head-on attacks during all bomb runs, an excellent job of bombing was accomplished and the other two combat wings that followed completed the work. The target was well and truly plastered, and was out of commission during the vital months that followed.

The battle of German aircraft production began with Oschersleben, it will continue until the end of the war, however there have been and will be other battles, i.e., the battle of oil production, transportation, and even support of our ground forces. We will win them and Jerry knows it.

4. It is recommended that all personnel of this command become familiar with the circumstances surrounding this mission as set forth herein.

By Command of Brigadier General
GROSS:
/s/ Vernon P. Smith
/t/ VERNON P. SMITH
1st Lt. Air Corps
Asst. Adjutant.

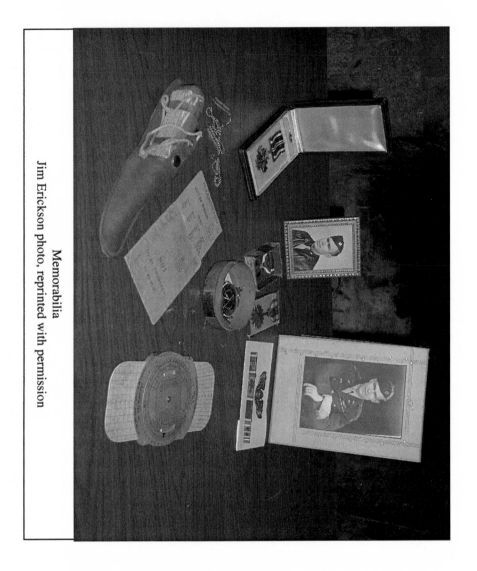

Memorabilia
Jim Erickson photo, reprinted with permission

Appendix B: Rapid Rewind

Realizing that Mission Memories only began with my military career and nothing about my previous life, I decided to add a brief outline between my birth and that period of my life.

1) Heritage
   a) Grandparents: all born in Norway – only maternal grandparents came to U.S.A.
   b) Parents: Father Arne Homdrom emigrated to U.S.A. at age 14. Mother Annie Vollen born on farm near Climax in Northwestern Minnesota
   c) Children: all born in Western North Dakota. After birth of 2 girls (Ruth, Gladys), 3 boys (Olaf, Theodore, Clarence) followed - Theodore being the next to the youngest, born on July 1, 1918
   d) Move to Minnesota: after father's death in 1921, mother moved with 5 children, ages 1 to 10, to Erskine in Northern Minnesota
2) Education
   a) Primary years
      i) First 3 years in 1 room. 1 teacher country school – a 3-mile walk each way.
      ii) Grades 4-8 in Erskine school after moving to our own small farm near the village.
   b) High school
      i) Gradually improved scholastically, finishing final year 2nd in class of 16.
      ii) Active in many extra-curricular activities such as basketball, singing and plays.
   c) College: Concordia College, Moorhead, MN:

      i) worked way through college, staying out 1 year to catch up on finances.

      ii) Graduated in 1941 with BA degree, majoring in history

      iii) Main activities were college plays, Concordia College Acapella choir (lowest 2nd bass), softball and horseshoe (champion)

3) Religion

   a) Baptized as a child in Lutheran Church, Williston, North Dakota

   b) Confirmation in Grace Lutheran Congregation, Erskine, 1933

   c) Sunday School every year before and after confirmation

   d) Youth League at Erskine

   e) Concordia College: regular attendance at church and daily chapel services as well as Luther League and Mission Crusaders.

4) Employment after graduating from Concordia College in May 1941

   a) Summer: farm work

   b) Autumn: teaching and coaching basketball – Comertown High School, Montana

5) Significant Historical Events

   a) December 7, 1941: Japan bombs Pearl Harbor

   b) US declares war on Japan, Germany and Italy (the Axis Powers)

   c) February 1942: drafted by the US Army from Ft. Snelling, Minnesota

   d) <u>Mission Memories</u>, World War II write-up continues the story of the author's life through that period from 1942 to 1945.

Appendix C: Fast Forward

Because it is over 55 years since I was involved in Missions in World War II, perhaps some readers would like to hear what I did after that. The title "Mission Memories" could cover another 35 years since then. What led up to further missions?

After my Honorable Discharge in mid 1945, I was offered the position of superintendent of the school that I left when I was drafted in 1942. However, I felt that with the GI Bill of Rights, I should rather go on to Graduate School at the University of Minnesota. It was a good year to get back into a more relaxing life. I sang in a very good church choir. I also met and dated many fine young women. At Lutheran Students Union I met Betty Stenberg, an undergraduate from Cass Lake, Minnesota. For the first time I felt that here was a person who would be an ideal mate for whatever direction my life took – even the possibility of the ministry! We were married in June 1946.

That fall I took a teaching position and basketball coaching in Ellsworth, Minnesota. The following year we became parents of our first child, Paul. During the summer I sensed more and more the call to the ministry. With Betty's strong support, I finally applied to go to Luther Seminary.

During those three years we had an open mind to any place the Lord would lead us to serve. In my final year the missions professor told the Foreign Mission Board that we had faithfully attended all the mission meetings. Consequently the Board called me in for an interview and asked if I would consider serving overseas. I replied that we would prayerfully consider it. Shortly thereafter we received a call to go to South

Africa. Simultaneously we received a call from the Home Mission Board to a parish in North Dakota.

In spite of many advantages such as being closer to relatives, a higher salary and better living conditions for remaining in America, we felt the greater need was overseas. By now we had a daughter Ev also, but at least there would be a few years until our children would have to attend school away from home. Also, unlike most seminary graduates who had some hesitation about the risks, I had already demonstrated my willingness to serve in extreme danger overseas. Thus after about three weeks we felt very strongly the Lord's leading to accept the call to the mission field. We left family and friends in November 1950 for a seven-year term.

I cannot possibly summarize in a few paragraphs our extraordinary experiences of those 35 years in South Africa. Perhaps my – or our – next writing task would be to continue under the same heading: "Mission Memories".

Notes

[1] See Appendix A

[2] Turner Publishing Company Staff. *Air Force Navigators Observers* 37

[3] Bishop, Cliff T. *Fortresses of the Big Triangle First* 95

[4] Smith, Graham. *Essex Airfields in the Second World War* 211

[5] MacKay, Ron. *381st Bomb Group* 22

[6] Stone, Ken. *Triumphant We Fly* 86

[7] MacKay 22

[8] Stone 91

[9] Ibid 88

[10] US Armed Forces Newspaper *US Stars and Stripes*, vol.4 No.61 (Jan.13, 1944)

[11] Brown, JG. *The Mighty Men of the 381st: Heroes All* 299

[12] Stone 94

[13] Brown 83

[14] T. Homdrom. Letters Home.

[15] MacKay 23

[16] John Burke. 1999 Interview at 381st Bomb Group Reunion.

[17] Society of the Strategic Air Command: America's Shield 13

[18] MacKay 26

[19] Brown 328ff

[20] *The American Heritage Picture History of World War II.* 419

[21] Brown 336

[22] Ibid 355

[23] Ibid 83

[24] Bishop 118

[25] Ibid 31

[26] Howland, John W *Diary of a Pathfinder Navigator* 58

[27] Honahan, Thomas L Interview at 1999 Reunion of 381st Bomb Group.

[28] MacKay 12

[29] Loc cit March 8, 1944

[30] MacKay 31ff

[31] Brown 374ff

[32] Bishop 124

[33] Ibid

[34] MacKay 35

[35] Stone 95

[36] MacKay 34

[37] Bishop 126

[38] MacKay 38

[39] *St. Paul Dispatch* March 15, 1944

[40] MacKay 39-41

[41] Brown 411

[42] Spielberg, Steven. "Saving Private Ryan"

[43] MacKay 45

[44] See appendix C

[45] DeLano, James. Interview at 1999 Reunion of 381st Bomb Group

[46] Ethall, J.L. *Bomber Command* 7

[47] Interview with his pilot, John H. Hallecy, at 1999 Reunion of 381st Bomb Group

[48] Coomer, John. *Combat Crew* 264

[49] Staff of Turner Publishing Co. *Air Force Navigators Observers* 92

Bibliography

The American Heritage Staff. *Picture History of World War II*. American Heritage Publishing Company, Inc. 1965.

Berdsall, Steve. *B-17 Flying Fortress Squadron*. Signal Publications Inc. (Carrollton, TX). 1986.

Bishop, Cliff T. *Fortresses of the Big Triangle First*. East Anglia Books (Bishops Stortford, England). 1986.

Brown, James G. *The Mighty Men of the 381st: Heroes All*. Publishers Press (Salt Lake City, UT). 1994.

Comer, John. *Combat Crew*. Texian Press (Waco, TX). 1986.

DeLano, James. Interview at 1999 Reunion of 381st Bomb Group, Texas.

Ethell, Jeffrey L. *Bomber Command*. Motorbook International (Osceola, WI). 1994.

Hallecy, John H. Interview at 1999 Reunion of 381st Bomb Group, Texas.

Homdrom, T. Letters Home.

Honahan, T. L. Interview at 1999 Reunion of 381st Bomb Group, Texas.

Howland, John W. *Diary of a Pathfinder Navigator*. 1999.

Letters from others.

MacKay, Ron *381st Bomb Group*. Squadron (Signal Publications, Inc. (Carrollton, TX) 1994

St. Paul Dispatch. About March 15, 1944.

Smith, Graham. *Essex Airfields in the Second World War*. Countryside Books (Newbury, Berkshire, England). 1996.

Society of the Strategic Air Command. *America's Shield*. Turner Publishing Co. (Paducah, KY). 1998.

Spielberg, Steven. "Saving Private Ryan". 1998.

Stone, Ken. *Triumphant We Fly: A 381st Bomb Group Anthology 1943-1945*. Turner Publishing Company (Paducah, KY). 1994.

Sulzberger, C.L. Editor. *American Heritage Pictorial History of World War II*. American. *Heritage Magazine US America*. ca 1964.

US Armed Forces Newspaper. *Stars and Stripes*. Vol.4. 1944.

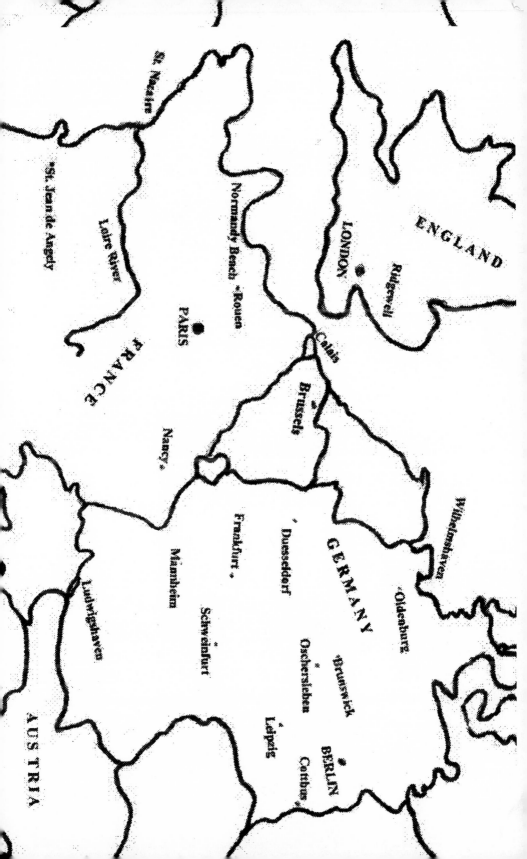